D1289989

LESBIANISM

an annotated bibliography and guide to the literature 1976–1991

by
DOLORES J. MAGGIORE

The Scarecrow Press, Inc.
Metuchen, N.J., & London
1992

Also by Dolores J. Maggiore from Scarecrow Press:

Lesbianism: An Annotated Bibliography and Guide to the Literature, 1976-1986 (1988)

British Library Cataloguing-in-Publication data available

Library of Congress Cataloging-in-Publication Data

Maggiore, Dolores J., 1947-
    Lesbianism : an annotated bibliography and guide to the
    literature, 1976-1991 / by Dolores J. Maggiore. -- [2nd ed.]
        p.   cm.
    Includes indexes.
    ISBN   0-8108-2617-8 (alk. paper)
    1. Lesbianism--United States--Bibliography. I. Title.
Z7164.S42M33   1992
[HQ75.6.U5]
016.303676'63--dc20   92-34699

CONTENTS

INTRODUCTION

We have come a long way since the Stonewall Riot in June 1969 when gays fought police harassment for the first time-- for their rights, for their protection, for their dignity. Today, in New York City, there is a gay rights bill which offers token shelter from discrimination in housing and employment. Why, then, is there a new aura of silence which surrounds the word "lesbian" and clouds the issues, pushing the lesbians back into the closet, and keeping heterosexuals in the helping professions ignorant of the oppression of gays due to invisibility?

In the context of fear surrounding AIDS and because of the thrust and implications of (Supreme Court) justice in Bowers vs. Hardwick (1986), where, in Georgia, privacy does not exist for homosexuals, gays and lesbians must allow themselves to be invisible. This minority group still lives in the shadow of ignorance that labels them sinners, criminals, or deviants. Only knowledge will allow gay people to step out of oppression, to see one another and to be seen.

As a social worker, one must recognize that potentially 10 percent of one's clients are gay. One must recognize, too, the special needs of this minority group.

Knowledge alone of the existence of gays does not suffice; ignorance of gay identity, gay lifestyles, gay families, etc., is tantamount to invisibility for gays. One cannot serve a population if it is not recognized.

Academic texts and university lectures urge social workers to recognize homosexuality and to examine one's feeling toward it. They do not, however, direct one to the information and the resources that will allow the worker to gain familiarity with gay people. Without information on gays, schools of social work cannot adequately prepare workers to encounter this population. It is this lack of knowledge, this invisibility, which prompted this researcher to compile this bibliography on lesbianism for social workers. Lesbians were chosen as the focus, separate from gay men, since lesbians have been the doubly invisible population among "homosexuals" or "gays." Much available data have merely been extrapolated from studies on gay men; once again, lesbians, as women, have been assumed into the general male image. The lesbian, then, must be recognized and understood. It is in the hope of improving service offered by social workers to the lesbian that this researcher has undertaken this bibliography and guide to the literature.

Dolores J. Maggiore
Centerport, New York

INTRODUCTION
TO THE 1992 EDITION

THE TRENDS OF THE YEARS 1987 - 1991

The writing of the 1988 edition of this work grew out of the paucity/dearth of social science material on lesbianism at the university where I was doing graduate work on Long Island, New York. After two years of research on ten years of literature (1976-1986), 300 pertinent articles were uncovered.

Now, four years later, in this second volume I have examined over 200 additional articles, dissertations, and books. These works were gleaned from a relative abundance of writing on lesbians and lesbian (and gay) issues, which caused me to further limit my search and to omit foreign and cross-cultural studies, literature on religion and spirituality and highly technical and/or narrowly specialized psychological, medical, and legal writings.

In general, there has been a wealth of material published by academic and lesbian and gay presses. Additionally, material is now more accessible to the general reader who will find articles on the lesbian (and gay) perspective on various issues in journals which do not specifically treat "gay" issues.

Yet, the bulk of this literature continues to focus on counseling and therapy. While there has been a proliferation of general "how to" (deal with lesbian clients) works, these works are somewhat elementary and address the needs of the therapist unfamiliar with gays and lesbians.

Literature on specific, more specialized issues in therapy with gays and lesbians is beginning to surface. Foremost among these issues, lesbian battering is being widely addressed by the lesbian and therapy communities which have produced excellent studies and treatment materials. Writers also speak more articulately about sex and not merely about sexual dysfunction.

Family issues have also seen a staggering increase in coverage, primarily in the legal arena of co-parenting and custody. More importantly, researchers are conceptualizing a new lesbian or gay family, one of choice.

Concerning minority issues, the literature on youth has also increased, while "aging" (lesbians) has been redefined from over 60 to 60s, to 50s, depending on the age of the researcher and as the "baby-boomers" mature, become respected professionals, and realize success.

Perhaps, if there is a theme to emerge from this (still) burgeoning literature on lesbian (and gay) studies, it is that this "baby-booming" field is maturing, growing more professional and realizing success. Works on lesbian history have multiplied. Titles on lesbian philosophy, psychology, mythology, and culture can be found in abundance.

Four years ago, it was argued that feminism was the "ism," the philosophy of the lesbian "movement." Gay men, unfortunately, lacked one, or, pretended the self-appointed politically correct lesbians, gay rights could be considered the "ism" of gay men. Sadly, AIDS became the major organizing factor (for lesbians too).

Now, theories and analysis envelop us, not just lesbians, but lesbians and gay men, as coalitions are built and a pluralistic perspective begins to take hold. This pluralism relates to a politic of inclusion among lesbians and among gay men and relates, as well, to lesbians and gay men together. It also extends to homosexualities to encompass a broader conceptualization of homosexuality.

Language is indeed being redefined by gays with far reaching and hard hitting societal implications. Writers speak of the lesbian or gay family and assume by that a constellation of (biological) family, of lovers, ex-lovers, friends, children, co-parents, whether lovers or not, gay men, sperm donors or actually psychological (and physical) fathers of their children, etc. These individuals may cohabit or not. Insurance companies and municipalities are beginning to respond. New York State saw its first lesbian co-adoption on January 31, 1992 and spousal benefits were awarded to the lesbian partner of a woman doctor by her Montefiore (Bronx, NY) hospital's own insurance in March of 1991.

Some of the old language is being retained. Scholars have returned to the word homosexuality, no longer viewing it as a clinical term which restricts and pathologizes lesbians and gays. Yet, they tend to talk about homosexualities, about the lesbians, gays, "queers," bisexuals, transvestites, transgenderists, etc. They describe individuals in terms of their sexual behaviors, and argue over the significance of self-labeling as lesbian or gay. *Sexual identity* and *preference* now take on different dimensions as emphasis moves from etiology to practice.

Certainly, some researchers still debate the nature/nurture question: Is one born gay or does one become gay? Is gayness "caused" by biology - something genetic - or does one's upbringing or later environment influence one to "become" gay? Although most researchers will admit of a combination of influences, Dr. Simon LeVay claims he has found the answer in the brain of the gay male. In 1991, his research showed the portion of the hypothalamus responsible for sexual activity to be smaller in homosexuals than in heterosexual men.

Despite the resultant renewal in the "born or bred" argument, the new philosophical argument is that of the essentialists versus the social constructionists. Is homosexual identity an essential identity or is it socially constructed? Has there always been a "lesbian identity" or is it a phenomenon of the late 19th and 20th centuries?

Activists and proponents of "identity politics" are adamant. They link "lesbian identity" with gay pride and community, as well as with protected (legal minority) status. Additionally, if the "cause" of one's lesbianism is genetic, then it is not one's "fault" if one is gay, and one must be protected under the law.

Social constructionists quote gender studies, and cross-cultural references. They are more likely to ask about the social and economic significance within 19th-century Lahaska society (native American) of a woman "berdache" (man-woman, third sex, woman in man's role) than about her sense of "lesbian identity." There is no direct, uninterrupted sense of history here.

Perhaps "queer" is an old word which more aptly describes past and present evolving "gay" history. Many lesbians have become more flexible in defining themselves. They're gay, maybe even "queer." They are in love with women; maybe they used to love men; maybe, they'll have a child with a gay man, etc. Some even admit to being involved sexually with straight men. Can they use the word "lesbian" to define themselves?

These are some of the issues encompassed by the new Gay Studies. It is a more scholarly, more grown-up, more recognized and acceptable field. It is reflective of a community which, it too, has become more visible, more recognized, more monied, more powerful. Gays are on the Phil Donahue and the Oprah shows. They're on the front page of the *New York Times* and the cover of *Newsday*. They have enough political clout to run two openly gay candidates for one City Council seat in New York City (1991). They have purchase power. They are indeed celebrities, wealthy people like Malcolm Forbes, "outed" by the publisher of a now defunct gay weekly *Outweek* as a gay celebrity who could have afforded to be visible as gay, and therefore effective in helping counteract homophobia.

As Gay Studies ages with some degree of sophistication, comfort, prosperity, and clout, so does the community. There are more study groups on racism, able-ism, classism, etc. There are more lesbians/gays involved in AIDS work and the gay rights fight. There are more lesbian and gay centers and bigger and better gay pride marches.

Yet, it seems that the gay and lesbian centers have very different functions for different groups. There are the $100 a plate dinners frequented by the established lesbians (and gays) and the poetry readings and movies attended by working class lesbians. Studies show a predominantly white, middle-class, suburban, educated sample. And national lesbian (and gay) groups solicit donations of $35 and up for one cause or another.

AIDS activists fight, too, over what population, what group, is doing the "real" AIDS work. Is Gay Men's Health Crisis, the foremost gay organization involved in AIDS work, really only attuned to white men? Is Speak Out, a national lobby group for gay rights, too "establishment"? Does Act Up, AIDS activists who believe in civil disobedience, better represent "queers" and all marginal peoples than legislative groups?

It becomes obvious that if these are the current struggles, Gay Studies and gays are vitally important in every aspect of life in the United States. Because of their high visibility, it is likewise easy to become complacent about this acceptance. One assumes it is becoming "okay" to be gay here, to have families here, to study here and work here, to build community and scholarship here, to *be* here.

And just as soon as this complacency begins to settle in, one is jolted as another story of skinheads, gay bashing, or a gay murder surfaces. Gay rights ordinances have been rescinded. Psychologists like Dr. Joseph Nicolosi claim curing or lessening the homosexual tendencies of clients. The State of Oregon whose capital, Portland, is a protected haven for lesbians and gays, is putting the "homosexual" question to a referendum in November 1992. Not only will "Measure 9" declare homosexuals to be sick and immoral, but it will instruct schools to teach this, and it will deny protection under the law to gays.

Thus, the rationale with which I began the 1988 edition, to find and record a body of literature on lesbians, to inform gays and straights, professionals and non-professionals, still exists. It is with renewed vigor that I affirm lesbians and lesbianism and the surge of lesbian creative activity that characterizes the years 1987-1991.

THE LITERATURE ON LESBIANISM OF THE YEARS 1987-1991

Concerning the section "The Individual Lesbian," history and culture dominate, and social constructionism is definitely the "buzz word." Wayne Dynes' 1990 *Encyclopedia of Homosexuality* is a compact version of "gay civilization."

The works of Faderman (1991), Duberman, Vicinus, and Chauncey (1989) represent excellent collections of articles about lesbianism (and gays) across time and culture. Altman, Vance, Vicinus, and Week (1988) have edited the papers on cross-cultural issues from the largest international conference on the homosexualities. Downing (1989) examines history and "same-sex love" among the Greek gods and goddesses, 19th-century psychoanalysts, Plato, and in the AIDS work of 20th-century America. Picking up the continuity/discontinuity theme in the telling of history, Ferguson (1990) speaks of the lack of international lesbian culture and calls for international lesbian movements which would eliminate "cultural imperialism."

In "Portraits," Risman and Schwartz (1988) and Stevens and Hall (1991) continue to speak about the medicalization of lesbianism and the evolution of myths concerning who lesbians are. Terry (1990) looks at "prejudiced" research conducted in the 1930s on the "masculine" woman because, at that time, there was no way to conceive of a (lesbian) woman as non-masculine if she was not attached to or had no point of reference to men. Hersch (1991) decries the rigid dichotomy gay-straight and tells lesbians to look rather at the quality of their loving and relationships.

Stage theories still represent the majority of articles listed under "Coming-Out." Chapman and Brannock (1987), Kahn (1991) and Froiden (1988) refer to CASS' stage theory of identity confusion, identity comparison, tolerance, acceptance, and pride. Franke and Leary (1991) study predictors of coming out and find one's "readiness" based more on anticipation of acceptance or rejection rather than on an internalized sense of self-acceptance.

The section on "Concept of Self" examines the individual and community. Once again, a social constructionist perspective influences Kitzinger (1988) who compares and contrasts feminism and liberal humanism, Phelan (1989) who writes on identity politics, and de Lauretis' (1991) collection of articles on lesbian culture. Pluralism is definitely the theme of the articles on philosophy and culture in Allen's (1990) excellent collection.

The "Minorities within a Minority" section is disappointing in the lack of a significant increase in articles on lesbians of color. Six articles cover the theme of doubly stigmatized identities: that of a lesbian and that of an ethnic. One author, Kanula (1990) refers to a third stigmatizing factor "battering" among black lesbians. There are additionally two anthologies by Latinas.

The same paucity is echoed in the articles on differently-abled lesbians (3), rural lesbians (1), and women in prison. This last article by Leger (1987) addresses the "importation/deprivation" controversy over lesbians in prison.

Concerning aging lesbians, "aging" is younger and younger. For Kehoe (1987), "aging" means over 60, for Gray (1987) over 50, while Sang, Smith and Warshow (1991) and Kirkpatrick (1989) study lesbians at "mid-life." Adelman (1990) has expanded her excellent earlier research and finds that greater life satisfaction was realized by gays who became aware of their gayness at an earlier age *and* who tended not to disclose their gayness or frequent gays. Galassi's (1991) excellent piece proposes an intergenerational model.

Literature on youth saw the greatest increase in volume. Many scholars acknowledge the need to identify gay youth and to get information out to them. Krysiak (1987) and Rofes (1989) speak of the role of schools and school counselors in identifying and servicing these adolescents. Paroski (1987) and Mercier-Berger (1989) suggest greater outreach to adolescents because their studies show that adolescents do not avail themselves of traditional and/or gay/lesbian services. Hunter (1990) and Hunter and Schaecher (1987) speak of depression and suicide attempts among adolescents. All researchers in this section, notably Browning (1987), Cates (1987), and Gonsiorek (1988) refer to the difficulty of mastering developmental tasks during adolescence when one is coping with a gay "IDENTITY" since integration of identity is the major task of adolescence. In general, writers speak of the need for family support and support groups. However, Solocinski (1990), in an excellent article, examines the ethics of a therapist discussing an adolescent's homosexuality with a parent. He explores the issue of the adolescent's competence and autonomy versus the need to involve a parent if/when the client is not deemed "competent."

Within the section on "Family," there are few additions to the works on family of origin or couples. In "Families of Procreation," the literature gained more perspective because of the presence of articles by two anthropologists -- Riley (1988) and Weston (1991). Both conceptualize gay families as families of choice as opposed to blood families. They challenge the hegemony of biology and develop political arguments for the acceptance (non-acceptance) by social institutions of this new concept of family. Essentially, friendship families would threaten the existing social, legal, and economic structures and thus, this idea of family will probably continue to be resisted.

Pollack and Vaughn (1987) and Bozett's (1987) collection of articles on all sorts of different family constellations and issues among gay families are well written. Pollack and Vaughn (1987) and Romans (1990) decry the literature which compares lesbian mothering to mothering by non-lesbians.

Family therapy is widely discussed and is represented by Crawford (1988) and Ross (1988) who present case studies of lesbian mothers and partners and teenage daughters. McCandlish (1987) and Evans (1990) discuss developmental theory for the co-parenting lesbian family (with adopted children or children by artificial insemination by donor), and Slater and Mencher (1991) speak of the "life cycle" and the absence of rituals in the lesbian family. Corley (1990) provides an excellent work on coming out to children. Bowen (1991) speaks of mothering as a black lesbian.

In the section on "Oppression," there are several good additions on civil rights. Most of the works, Arriola's (1988), Siegel's (1991), Bersoff and Ogden's (1991) refer to the privacy and equal protection arguments used in gay rights cases. These are also well developed in Granger's (1991) article on "Outing." There is an excellent review of case law by the Editors of the Harvard Law Review (1990), and Mohr (1988) and Kirk and Madsen (1989) basically deal with strategies for gaining gay rights. Mohr calls for civil disobedience. Kirk and Madsen downplay the importance of lobbying for legislation and demonstrations. They suggest a media campaign which creates the message that it's not fashionable to be prejudiced and discriminatory. Ettelbrick (1991) addresses practical protection of one's goods and family: wills, powers of attorney, co-habitation, co-parenting contracts, etc. Additionally, Duffy (1991) writes on the defense of battered lesbians who attack their batterers.

Custody has received good coverage in the past five years. Achtenberg (1987) and (1991) and Erlichman (1989) dispel myths about (parenting) lesbians while Falk (1989) and Gibbs (1989) review the literature and studies comparing lesbian and non-lesbian mothers. Arnup (1989) examines the history and evolution of custody laws (in Canada).

Family is redefined by Poverny and Finch (1988) who write on domestic partnerships. The strength of the lesbian family is celebrated by Polikoff (1987) and Pollack (1987) who criticize studies which describe lesbian mothering as "as good" (as that of non-lesbian mothering). Polikoff sees the practicality of arguing in this fashion in court but presents lesbian and gay lawyers with the challenge

of not compromising gay families and their own integrity as
gay lawyers.

Lewin (1990) presents a rationale for avoiding
custody fights and suggests that by not depending on her ex-
husband, a lesbian curtails his power over her and her
children, builds her own autonomy, and changes
motherhood from a biologically assumed and attributable
characteristic which could be denied if she is unfit in court to
a consciously achieved characteristic. Hitchens (1990)
suggests excellent preparation strategies for a custody case.
Di Lapi (1989) also describes the conflict in identity for
lesbians who are mothers and the motherhood"hierarchy."
She warns professionals not to perpetuate this oppression by
comparing lesbian to non-lesbian mothering.

In the area of "Health," the absence of certain studies
in gynecological health is more noteworthy than what is
actually new. However, Hitchcock's (1989) bibliography
on women's health issues is important. While there are two
or three articles on AIDS, all are already out of date as far as
safer sex for lesbians is concerned. Rieder and Ruppelt's
(1988) collection of articles on women and AIDS and their
significant others has a chapter which deals specifically with
lesbians, and lesbians are widely represented among the
contributors. Reyes' (1991) politicized article is also
noteworthy.

There are no studies on breast or cervical cancer, and
the only other pertinent and political article is that by Shaw
(1989) decrying the underreporting of lesbians among
women with certain illnesses, and therefore, the lack of
studies, funding, and treatment.

Concerning alcoholism, there is much that is new but little that is innovative: general reviews of literature and articles stating the need for workers to familiarize themselves with gay issues, and the need for alcoholism treatment and psycho (dynamic) therapy. There is one article on alcoholism and sex abuse by Neisen and Sandall (1990), one on alcoholism and violence (1990) by Schilit and Lie, and several pamphlets on recovery and gays by Hazelden and a book by Black (1990) on gays and ACOA (adult children of an alcoholic) issues.

Concerning therapy, most of the work deals with familiarizing therapists new to lesbian clients with the world of the lesbian. Silverstein's (1990) and Rothblum and Cole's (1989) collection are excellent exceptions. Well-written and well-balanced as to the nature of the therapeutic issues discussed, each is representative of some of the finest therapy written up. The Boston Lesbian Psychology Collective (1987) also provides an excellent collection of pertinent articles on a wide range of clinical issues including battering and the instances of incest among lesbians.

Specific areas of therapy receive some attention. The article on bereavement by Martin (1991) is a must for all bereavement counselors, especially because of the astute, sensitive treatment of transference and countertransference. Rice (1990) writes on eating disorders and Saunders and Valente (1987) on suicide, while Frye (1990), Loulan (1988 and 1989) and Rothblum and Brehony (1991) address issues of sex, sexuality, and sex therapy. Frye and Rothblum and Brehony address the alleged lack of sex in lesbian relationships, while Loulan celebrates the erotic. Hamadock (1988) writes about how a therapist can introduce dialogue about sex as an important part of a lesbian's life even when sex is not *the* issue. The notion of "dysfunction" is absent from all of this literature.

Concerning couples, Green (1990), Mitchell (1989), Pearlman (1989), and Rotenberg (1989) discuss intimacy and merger. Merger is no longer seen as the shibboleth of the 1970s and 1980s, but rather as a coping mechanism to deal with homophobia. Writers contrast it with fusion which they see as indicative of a lack of ego boundaries.

The treatment of battering in the lesbian community is, by far, the area which has received wide and deep coverage. Sorely needed, works by Schilit, Clarke and Shallenberger (1988), and Lie and Gentlewarrier (1991) acknowledge that battering, indeed, does exist and base their findings on studies and surveys. Leeder (1988) and Klinger (1991) especially provide excellent case studies and in-depth treatment plans including those for the batterer as well. An excellent emotionally charged general overview of battering is provided by the Lesbian Caucus of the Massachusetts Coalition for Battered Women (1990). Their thirty minute tape is a must. Hammond (1988), Leeder (1988), and Renzetti (1989) speak to the need for outreach and sensitive workers since lesbians are not welcomed in women's shelters. Lawyers, like Duffy (1991), are even addressing the issue of defending lesbians who attack and harm their batterers.

Many of the gaps in the literature from 1976-1986 have been filled in the past five years. Still missing are the studies of children born through AID (artificial insemination by donor) to lesbian mothers and in-depth studies of lesbian families. AIDS and breast cancer in lesbians need to be addressed, including up-to-date information on safer sex for lesbians. Studies must include African-American, Asian-American, Latina, differently-abled, rural lesbians, etc. If, politically, these groups choose not to participate in studies conducted by white, middle class, able-bodied lesbians, then, perhaps collectives or coalitions of "minority" groups could undertake representative studies. Concerning therapy, there is a need for further studies on eating disorders.

Finally, writers need to find a way to salvage the lesbian (and gay) resources which are disappearing. Bookstores are closing. For example, New York City, Long Island, and the greater metropolitan area no longer have a lesbian bookshop. Newspapers of long standing like *Gay Community News* are folding, as are weeklies like *Outweek*. Additionally, some mail-order bookshops often fail to list academic and hard-bound books. If lesbians are to continue to inform and to teach, vehicles to implement this dissemination must be kept alive.

AN OVERVIEW OF THE FINDINGS

The bibliography includes more than three hundred and fifty abstracts, annotations, and resources. The original books or articles in this study were written or published from 1976 through 1986, and every effort has been made to include those works published as late as fall 1986. This researcher has chosen to limit the study to the past ten years out of a concern for accuracy and validity. Yet, some of the earlier works in the field of psychology and psychiatry still reflect a tendency to view lesbianism as an illness, as if the decision had not been made to remove it from the *Diagnostic and Statistical Manual of Mental Disorders* (D.S.M.) in 1973. Despite the abundance of titles, the reader with a limited amount of time may still gain insightful, working knowledge of lesbians and lesbianism since the researcher has marked with an asterisk (*) those works which exemplify the best in each category.

The works are all nonfiction and have been selected from fields ranging from social work, sociology, and psychology to law, contemporary women's literature, and feminist social analysis. Contained in this study are the results of empirical studies, as well as judicial decisions and political theory. Some works claimed to be important are blatantly missing from this study since they deal exclusively with gay men or merely generalize findings to include lesbians. A judicious effort has been made to exclude any works whose perspective on lesbianism is negative or contains erroneous information. Unfortunately, some very valid works have been omitted since they are currently out of print or can be located only with great difficulty in specialized collections or archives. Notable among the omissions are works by Baba Copper on aging, Marilyn Fleener on lesbian lifestyle, and Hornstein and Fifield on lesbian health issues.

The works have been classified according to five general topics:

The individual lesbian, covering issues of identity throughout history and in the current variety of lifestyles, and of self-labeling in coming out and in the construct of self-concept;

Minorities within a minority, ranging from lesbians of color to rural lesbians and "differently-abled" (handicapped) lesbians;

Lesbian families, including families of orientation, lesbian couples, and families of procreation;

Oppression, examined as heterosexism in theory and heterosexism in practice, in the courts, in the workplace, and in the general denial of civil rights;

Special health issues, both gynecological and mental, with a focus on alcoholism and counseling.

Organizations relevant to the topic are included at the end of each section. Moreover, a final section on resources is included in order to direct social workers to general guides, directories, and newspapers that list calendars of lesbian and feminist events, as well as to feminist, gay, and lesbian bookstores where materials and knowledge of other groups and events may be procured.

An inspection of the bibliographic entries by subtopic indicates a general scarcity of titles on rural lesbians and differently-abled lesbians.   Moreover, while there is a growing literature of lesbians of color, little or no empirical information is available on them. Empirical studies are likewise missing on lesbian youth and, to a lesser degree, on lesbian couples. These populations would seem, then, to be among the most "secret" (Simmel, cited in Ponse, 1978), when one considers the surveys administered and questionnaires returned. On the other hand, it is only recently that numerous studies have been conducted among aging lesbians, once considered a truly invisible population. Many of the new titles released from 1984 to 1986 do, in fact, deal with lesbians and aging. That studies have been made at all is no small feat because of the fear of disclosure of "secret" populations.

This fact, too, has rendered much of the research on lesbianism skewed toward the white, middle-class, activist lesbian. This polling of "secret" populations is the major cause of difficulty in obtaining true samplings.

One other area receiving greater notice now is that of lesbian (and gay) parenting. Several works have recently been published on the topic of artificial insemination by donor (AID) and other means of parenting, such as adoption and foster parenting. In conjunction with this, then, is a growing emphasize on legal matters, contractual agreements, and legal rights in general.

I. THE INDIVIDUAL LESBIAN

LESBIAN IDENTITY

This section on identity will examine who the lesbian is. It seeks to view her first from an historical and then from a contemporary perspective. The lesbian's presence in history affects the way society currently sees her and the way she sees herself. The manner in which she sees herself will be treated as self-labeling. It includes her coming-out process, that is, the evolution of her self-acceptance as a lesbian and her concept of self.

History

Even a cursory glance at the titles on lesbian history will reveal a paucity of material. This very lack of material is consistent with the thrust of the researchers' focus: lesbians are all but invisible in history. Because of the cultural need to recognize one's reference group in history in order to identity and take pride in that identity, lesbians are examining the past in search of their roots. Who are the lesbians of the past? What has shaped their culture? Who has hidden traces of their presence and why?

The central theme of the current histories and historical research being compiled is the utter obliteration of lesbianism in an effort to protect heterosexism. Schwarz (1979), Faderman (1981), and Duggan (1979) describe this form of social control which has kept other women ignorant of the existence of lesbianism and ignorant of its inherent challenge to patriarchal values. If historians have alluded to lesbianism at all, they have named it something else. According to Duggan (1979), the writing of lesbians into history would have provided the proof of their existence and the role models necessary for the easier assertion of one's lesbian identity. Faderman (1981) writes that only at the turn of the twentieth century, upon the emergence of greater independence for women, was "intimate friendship" between women seen as sexual or as a threat to male privilege. Financially independent and sexually and emotionally fulfilled women could feasibly do without men.

Portraits

The current histories, then, are attempting to identify lesbianism, lesbians, and lesbian culture from the past. In so doing, they shape and refine definitions of what it means to be a lesbian. Already this historical contest provides the descriptions of "independent woman" and "woman involved in intimate friendship." Sociological researchers attempt to come to a more narrow definition of the word "lesbian" and encounter great difficulty because of the diversity within the lesbian world. Further complications set in when one considers who (the lesbian herself, the lesbian community, or heterosexual society) is attaching the label "lesbian," and what (identity, behavior, or feelings) is being labeled.

"Women-identified woman" is a definition used by the Radicalesbians, a political group of lesbian separatists, in an early 1970s work. It has been interpreted to mean women for whom other women are their primary emotional, erotic, and spiritual attachments. According to Schwarz (1979), Browning (1984), and Demming (1981), this definition would include women who have rejected patriarchy. For some lesbians, this rejection is a conscious political act, an embracing of radical feminism, a defiant "no" to women's traditional sex roles. For others, the political significance is not willful, but rather their "gayness" is a refusal to play the role of wife and sexual partner to a man.

In addition to the emphasis on definitions of lesbianism, researchers examine the diversity among lesbians. Coming from various ethnic, racial, class, and geographical backgrounds, lesbians are also married, divorced, widowed, single, or in couples, mothers, monogamous, nonmonogamous, conservative, liberal, radical, etc. Lewis (1979) describes some differences between lesbians pre-1955 and after. The pre-1955 lesbian tends to be more closeted and less political; perhaps she is among the less than 20 percent of lesbians (composite percentage) found to "role play." Belote and Joesting (1976) and Lehman (1978) also find little evidence of role playing among lesbians, and Lehman stresses differences in this area between lesbians and gay men. Likewise, in the place of other myths concerning deviance and sickness, researchers Belote and Joesting (1976), Demming (1981), and Loewenstein (1980) present a portrait of a healthy, independent woman, identifying and loving in a positive manner with other women.

SELF-LABELING

Coming Out

How does one come to a sense of lesbian identity? Who decides whether one is a lesbian? And what aids in the positive self-identification as a lesbian? "Coming out" is the process by which one moves toward a lesbian identity, adopts and adapts some of, all of, or none of the definitions and aspects of lesbianism reflected in and by other lesbians and heterosexual society. Researchers describe the process of coming out as one of awareness and acceptance, a choice, according to Weitz (1984), in response to a sexist society. For Baetz (1984), coming out entails crossing over a "culturally constructed mine field intended to eliminate or impede the lesbian lifestyle" (p. 45). She addresses the issue of the violence to which one exposes oneself at each new stage of coming out. In coming out, one risks a loss of self-esteem, of confidence, or of socioeconomic privilege by a hostile heterosexist world. Even in therapy, the lesbian may experience "violence" in the therapist's trivialization of what the lesbian faces, or by the therapist's not challenging the lesbian's potentially internalized self-hatred. Interactionists Elliott (1985), Browning (1984), and Gramick (1984) speak of the assigning and modification of meaning attached to one's developing sexuality as one interacts with other lesbians. In general, the researchers refer to the process as one of stages, whereby one first experiences feelings of difference (signification), then an attraction to the same sex (awareness), then interaction with other lesbians, and finally self-acceptance. Gramick (1984) stresses that usually there is a need for a long-term relationship or involvement in more than one relationship in order to fully accept one's lesbian identity. Ponse (1978) describes the "gay trajectory" in a somewhat similar fashion, but she precedes the seeking out of involvement in the community and in a relationship by a general acceptance of one's feelings and of the implications for one's identity.

On the other hand, Sophie's (1986) research with fourteen lesbians indicates that not one of the stage theories is consistent with their experiences of coming out. The difficulty, she believes, stems from the linear nature of the stage theory. In addition, she voices a disclaimer as to her methodology in choosing the sample. Obtaining true samplings will be a concern throughout the various studies.

Contrary to this general trend of proceeding inductively, Faderman's (1984) theory of the coming-out process progresses deductively. She claims that a woman makes a critical examination of society, that is, experiences a universal sensitivity to oppression. She is then moved to a sociocentric stage where she feels alienated by patriarchy and isolated when she remains outside the women's community. Finally, it is in the egocentric stage where this politically aware woman may or may not become involved in a lesbian relationship. Regardless of the sexual behavior, Faderman holds that this woman has come to a self-acceptance as a lesbian woman.

Inconsistent with this emphasis on positive identity and on the meaning attached by the woman herself to the behavior and feelings is the critique of feminism and lesbianism by DeFries (1979). She sees feminism as an artificial, external factor which prompts a premature self-declaration of the "still uncertain" sex inclination and as a justification for one's sexuality. Moreover, she dismisses political lesbianism as an uncritical adoption of an ideology, causing one to deprive oneself of the support of the prevailing (heterosexual) ideology which would allay one's fears of difference.

A final note of concern is voiced by Valverde (1983), who urges lesbians to be aware of differing circumstances that facilitate or hinder one's coming out. Some lesbians lack the wherewithal to risk exposing themselves by coming out publicly. In one's spontaneous and political need to be visible as a lesbian, one must not jeopardize the position of those for whom the risk of loss is too great.

Concept of Self

Learning to deal with difference, and therefore, to alter, to adapt, or to conform one's concept of self is addressed quite adeptly in a few select sociological and psychological studies. The researchers examine the construct of self-concept within the context of heterosexual society and the lesbian community. A shaping facet of this development is the lesbian's awareness of her minority status in a world which stigmatizes her, a stigma which she may internalize to a greater or lesser degree.

The works of Ponse (1978), Brooks (1981), and McCoy and Hicks (1979) all focus on the theme of the construct of self-concept and identity and the lesbian community. The controversy and the dilemma for the individual lesbian results from questions of which identity, lesbian or personal, should be emphasized, and whether, in fact, there is an actual conflict between the two.

For McCoy and Hicks (1979), this question of personal or individual identity versus group (lesbian) identity is essentially a matter of a balance of power. In a society hostile to that which threatens patriarchy, the lesbian seeks and receives support and safety within the lesbian community. This is the network of lesbian organizations, institutions, and friends that forms a subculture or a community for the lesbian. According to McCoy and Hicks, the individual lesbian feels a pull between "membership" in the community and an individual life outside the group in a society which stigmatizes her and offers her no validation. The individual who does not seem to fit completely and collectively risks being rejected or fears this rejection to a hostile, oppressive society. The community is seen as all-powerful since it has the power to reject. The individual lesbian woman, socialized as a woman not to have power and angered by this lack of power and control, may often strike back at the members of the community as mirror images of self. Just as a power balance must be struck within the community, so too, the individual must find and assert the power within herself. Moreover, she must seek the balance between her group identity and her personal identity, between merger with the group and total autonomy.

In a similar vein, Brooks (1981) discusses affiliation as potential compartmentalization of self. She, too, refers to "membership" in the community as positive identification, as going beyond the negative stereotypes and thus overcoming stigma. However, in an effort to avoid devaluation and, therefore, powerlessness, lowered self-esteem, and an inability to cope, she may subordinate all other roots of self-identity to her group or lesbian identity. This may result, says Brooks, in compartmentalization, in people's seeing only one part of her. In heterosexual society, she is expected by non-gays to cover up or deny her sexuality; whereas, in the lesbian community, "she may be accepted exclusively because of it" (p. 138). Furthermore, according to Krieger (1982) commenting on Brooks, "a lesbian identity may represent a fused identity against which personal identity must repeatedly be asserted" (p. 236).

A theme which is focused upon by Ponse (1978) and which is also the focus of Brooks' work is the rejection, redefining, and restructuring of the label or identity attributed to the lesbian by others. In the case of Brooks, this label is stigma, the message that heterosexuality is the only way and that homosexuality is bad and sick. Dissonant with the values and the position of majority society, homosexuality is often trivialized and reduced to mere sexuality. The majority assumption is one of superiority and righteousness. Reduced to sexuality, homosexuality is no real threat to the majority. Lesbians, according to Brooks, must reject the assumption that the only difference between lesbians and non-lesbians is sex. By asserting her identity and providing new information (cognitive restructuring), the lesbian redefines and reinforces her concept of self, and changes the meaning of the external (and indirectly) the internal stress. The result is an increase in self-esteem and coping skills.

A final note on Brooks' perspective on identity is her call for visibility. She claims that by identifying and by standing out as a lesbian, an individual joins with other lesbians and moves to a collective restructuring of stress. Within the collective, she calls for diversity in order to avoid factionalism, which can only lead to tokenism or a continued repression or disregarding of the isolated factions of small numbers remaining visible.

The same themes of personal versus lesbian identity, the redefinition of meaning, and the power of the definer are studied by Ponse (1978). She focuses on the labeling of the lesbian by both the heterosexual world and the lesbian community. In an effort, she says, to prevent cultural dissonance, both groups attach the label "lesbian" (although of different signification) to the woman whose behavior fits her into this mold. The heterosexual world, then, sees her as essentially sick because her behavior, reduced to sexuality, is consistently deviant from the norm. The lesbian community urges one to "come out" in order to expand oneself to one's full lesbian identity and overcome this stigma. Because of the security and validation offered by the community, the individual often bonds closely with the group that becomes the "norm-setting" vehicle for the definition of individual lesbian identity.

Ponse rejects this polarity of identity, heterosexual or lesbian, based on the equating of identity solely with activity. In opposition to these labeling theories, she stresses self-designation or redefinition by the lesbian herself. While cognizant of the constraints put on the lesbian by others, Ponse claims that the power over one's own fate must lie with the individual. Lesbianism, she claims, is a pervasive identity, a matter of being and becoming as well as of having been. Important in the construct of this identity, then, is the meaning which the individual herself attaches to the feelings, activities, and identity. The individual has the ability and the power to develop a "quasi-independent" definition of self, a definition which she may reject, refine, or change. Ponse, therefore, would include within her label of lesbian the following four typologies: women who identity as lesbians and whose activity is lesbian; women who identity as lesbian, but whose activity is bi-sexual; women who identify as bi-sexual, but whose activity is exclusively lesbian; and women who identify as heterosexual, but whose activity is lesbian.

Based on the information in this section of the individual lesbian and identity, one may conclude that there is a need for further research by women, lesbian and/or heterosexual, about lesbians. More historical study will reveal more role models and add greater dimension to the heritage. Truer samplings can only present a more varied and culturally authentic portrait and coming-out process for all lesbian women in the United States. Finally, although this section has concentrated on the individual lesbian, researchers must delve into the question of the individual within the group. Krieger (1982) urges greater study on the internal dynamics of the lesbian community and its connection to lesbian identity. Needed too, are the studies on various lesbian communities across neighborhood, ethnic, racial, and class lines. According to Krieger, the opportunity is here to study the development of the female identity in an all-female society and the individual in a community of likeness.

II. MINORITIES WITHIN A MINORITY

LESBIANS OF COLOR/THIRD WORLD LESBIANS

"Difference within a community of sameness" repeats a theme previously discussed in the section on the individual lesbian and identity. The major focus of the works dealing with third world lesbians or lesbians of color can be summarized as a question of ethnic or lesbian "majority status." Writers refer to a conspiracy of silence, one which would separate the "ethnic" from the white as well as the heterosexual woman from the lesbian woman. In the more conservative ethnic or third world community, homosexuality is often seen as the "white disease," as genocide at the hands of the whites, and as an affront to third world nationalism (Cornwell, [1983]; Smith, [1981]; Jones, [1983]). In the case of Cuban lesbians, lesbianism is associated with pre-Castro capitalist corruption or a detraction from one's revolutionary spirit. T h e homosexuality of (now) expatriate Cubans has even been exploited and their politics undermined by the C.I.A. and right-wing Cubans under the guise of supportive action for civil rights for homosexuals. In truth, the mechanism at play is the forced choosing of one's national politics over one's sexual politics. Likewise, Monteflores (1981) speaks of a "primary identity," that is, the greater identification with one's ethnic identity or one's lesbianism. Jones (1983), too, states that third world youth tend to identify more with their ethnic or racial identity than with a gay identity. According to Clarke (1981), separation impedes a joint struggle of white and black lesbian women united against the colonist, the man. Clarke claims that maleness is all that was left to black men, who, in turn, subjugate "their" women. Lesbianism, as an attack on colonialism, can be the unifying factor for black and white lesbians. This, then, is Clarke's answer to racism, which, like homophobia, has been internalized by all, even the lesbian community.

Once again one is reminded to make the connection between the oppressions: that racism, sexism, and classism stem from the same root, that is, from heterosexism. Lorde (1983) refers to multi-oppressions and urges that one cannot allow any one part to be oppressed over the other. Those who suffer oppression as people of color, as women, and as lesbians, cannot choose one oppression over another. Likewise, one cannot allow any group to be oppressed while one fights another oppression. One has to fight oppression. The trend among third world lesbians and lesbians of color, then, is to refuse to deny difference, but also to refuse to choose one oppression over the other. Noda, Tsui, and Wong (1979) urge Asian lesbians to come out as third world women within the lesbian community and as lesbians within the third world. Anzaldua and Moraga (1981) also present a portrait of the third world woman or woman of color who stands out and receives and gives her strength and validation in her visibility as a third world lesbian. Strength gained in the struggle for lesbian rights can only profit the movement for third world rights and vice versa. Hidalgo (1984) speaks of the high level of political activism both as lesbians and as Puerto Ricans among her sample. Native Americans Cameron (1981) and Brant (1984) are also standing out in the struggle for gay rights. One is urged to use difference, to confront and acknowledge it. In an effort to find common ground, Lorde (1983) advises women to profit from one another's difference to form a richer vision. Thus, the direction of the future would seem to lie in coalitions of difference and not in a leveling of difference.

AGING

An invisible or less visible minority is that of the aging lesbian. Some would prefer to be called old; yet, this depends on one's cohort. Most research focuses on the profile of the older lesbian (age 50+) and advantages and disadvantages to aging as a lesbian. Lesbian theory in this area centers around the issue of ageism as yet another oppression stemming from heterosexism.

Researchers consistently draw the portrait of a well-adjusted, active woman. Many older lesbians are involved in committed relationships where they continue to be sexually active. Most have well-developed friendship networks, which researchers, especially Wolf (1978), hold accountable for their generally high level of well-being. According to Wolf, friends take the place of family for the older lesbian, who most probably does not enjoy a positive relationship with her family of origin. Raphael and Robinson (1981) also find that the lesbian's relationship with her family depends on the degree of her overtness. These images contrast sharply with the traditionally held view of the unhappy, isolated, bitter lesbian. In only one instance, researchers Martin and Lyon (1979) refer to the isolated lesbian from their earlier work *Lesbian Woman*.

Studies conclude that lesbians may, in fact, have the advantage over non-lesbians in certain aspects of aging. Researchers agree that because she has had to cope with stigma and find alternative means of dealing in a hostile world, the lesbian may be better able to cope with aging.

Laner (1979) claims that the lesbian does not experience acceleration of aging, does not seek out younger partners, and actually enjoys a much wider range of potential partners than does the heterosexual woman. Berger (1982) also addresses the issue of the heterosexual woman's outliving her husband and being alone at an earlier age. Where no discrepancy in life expectancy between the sexes exists, partners in a lesbian dyad or potential social companions/lovers are less likely to lose one another to an earlier death. Laner adds that if a partner does die or leave, the lesbian, never having been cut off from the lesbian community, remains in touch with a network of companions, friends, and potential mates/lovers.

A criticism of the would-be security of the lesbian community is voiced by radical lesbians Copper (1985) and MacDonald and Rich (1983). They view the community as having internalized the ageism which is prevalent in (American) society. Ageism separates younger lesbians from older lesbians, stratifies them into mother and daughter roles, and perpetuates a patriarchal model of self-effacement and enslavement. Lesbians, then, who look to one another as mother/daughter/grandmother have internalized the message that only the young, productive, sexy woman of use to the patriarchy is needed, accepted, or allowed to be visible. Young lesbians cannot expect old lesbians to sacrifice themselves again as the all-giving mothers. Copper calls for a self-examination to root out one's own internalized ageism, for an integration of all lesbians as useful, active, egalitarian members, and for a community-wide campaign against ageism.

If ageism within the lesbian community is a reflection of the ageism in society, what services are provided by a patriarchal society to an aging lesbian woman? Senior citizen centers do exist; however, no specific provision is made for lesbian seniors. Moreover, these services are actually vastly underutilized by lesbians, perhaps out of a fear of disclosure. Nursing homes, when they do accept acknowledged or overt homosexuals, will usually accept only one partner if a couple is involved. Visitation rights in intensive care units are restricted to immediate family, which is likewise entrusted with decision-making powers in life-death matters. Other legal worries of older lesbians involve wills and inheritance of jointly owned goods.

Lesbians in the studies voice some concern over retirement. Lesbians show great interest in a retirement home for gays (men and women) together, as well as an increasing interest in collective living. Many women express a desire for collectivity within their age cohort; others want a more age-integrated community. Almvig (1982) currently heads a group, Matrix, working on the establishment of a retirement home for lesbians. The presence of S.A.G.E. (N.Y.), an integrated social, political, and educational group for older (and younger) gays, exists as a positive affirmative action for, by, and with older lesbians and gays.

Future study, according to Robinson (1979), might focus on this expressed need for alternatives in retirement living. In addition, the long-term relationships of older lesbians should be examined to reflect changes in societal values and the time period of development as an adult. Having grown up as a lesbian in the 1940s is a totally different experience from having matured as a lesbian in the 1960s. Additionally, Robinson says that if a developmental model is to be created as a framework against which to view the lesbian, it must consider the roles she has or has not experienced due to her lesbian lifestyle. Perhaps, if the lesbian has never married, she has neither children nor in-laws.

YOUTH

Just as ageism impedes the full integration of the older lesbian into society and sometimes within the lesbian community, ageism also keeps lesbian youth separate and invisible as lesbians. The greatest problem for lesbian youth would seem to be one of isolation and alienation. This alienation is very often witnessed in its most abject state, that of the lesbian runaway. Most writers and researchers in this section on lesbian youth focus on gay runaways, who, according to Gibson (cited in Bergstrom and Cruz, 1983), account for approximately 25 percent of the youth serviced by Huckleberry House, a runaway youth shelter in San Francisco. Many of these young people have been thrown out by parents or have run away to escape abuse. Often, they are abusing drugs and alcohol and have turned to prostitution to support themselves. As a result, their self-esteem is so closely tied to their ability to "service" others that they often cannot relate to adult counselors in other than a seductive way. Moreover, there exists a barrier of general distrust resulting from their victimization by rape, incest, and/or general abuse.

Housing, shelters, and safe environments are the greatest needs consistently indicated by the researchers. Shelters do not willingly accept openly lesbian youth. If it is discovered that the youth is lesbian, she is often harassed, abused, and accused of being disruptive. The end result is that she is discharged back to an abusive home or the street. Likewise, foster parents are often insensitive or abusive to the overt lesbian. Given a history of expulsion, the lesbian youth may not avail herself of services even where they do exist. Nor is the lesbian community easily accessible or welcoming to her, since an adult lesbian runs the risk of legal problems even for renting an apartment to her (a minor).

Rejected by both worlds and deprived of role models, the lesbian youth experiences a complicated identity crisis. Socialized as a young woman, the lesbian youth has probably had little sexual exposure to either sex, according to Rose's work (cited in Bergstrom and Cruz, 1983). She may have internalized negative stereotypes of lesbian women, and without role models she may act out what she believes a lesbian to be. In counseling these young lesbians, youth workers agree on the need to be supportive and tolerant of this potentially exaggerated behavior. Trust has to be established to bridge the isolation. A counselor must reach for the young lesbian's self-disclosure of sexuality in a way which is accepting of sexual activity in general and allows her to feel the worker's supportiveness of her lesbianism or bisexuality should she choose to reveal it.

Workers recommend family counseling, if possible, or the creation of "extended families" (non-kin) in lieu of biological families. In addition, the runaway may require training, including academic, vocational, and/or career.

Outside the concrete need for housing, the young lesbian is also in need of workers sensitized to the issue. The employment of gay and lesbian workers to serve as positive role models and the training of non-gay staff can provide great service where little currently exists. There is an overwhelming need for outreach to these young lesbians, as well as to sensitive individuals, gay or straight, to act as supportive foster parents. Shelters must be created or converted specifically to meet the needs of lesbian (and gay) youth, and funding sought to underwrite programs designed to service this often invisible, isolated population.

DIFFERENTLY-ABLED LESBIANS

Another population which suffers triple stigma and yet, at times, remains invisible is that of differently-abled lesbians. Very little information accessible to the general public is available. It seems that this population, too, has been made to choose its oppression: identity as a lesbian or as a differently-abled woman. Moreover, there are those whose disability is not visible and are therefore assumed to be able-bodied. Writers agree on the triple stigma of being a differently-abled or physically-challenged lesbian woman in an able-bodied heterosexist world.

Given the lack of accessibility to many buildings and to means of transportation and the presence of physical barriers in general, the removal of the differently-abled from the view of the able-bodied functions as an even greater psychological separation. Nestle (1981) speaks of the societal tendency to blame the victim in a society whose laxness on environmental controls and standards should be examined and analyzed. Authors refer to the group work on anger and frustration present in this population and describe the therapeutic process as one of dealing with loss. One grieves the loss of lovers and friends to illness, the loss of sexual function or treatment as asexuals by the able-bodied, the loss of self-esteem and rights guaranteed able-bodied and/or heterosexual people. Rubin (1981) addresses the important issues of the mobility, duration and progression of illness, as well as the abject fear of discovery of one's lesbianism by families on whom some differently-abled lesbians are solely dependent.

From the brevity of this report, it is obvious that more research is necessary. Greater visibility for the differently-abled can only serve to raise the consciousness of those ignorant of the oppression of able-ism or unaware of the magnitude of the problem.

RURAL LESBIANS

Lack of visibility is, at once, the greatest problem and perhaps, according to some, the most secure position for the rural lesbian. The lack of information available confirms the fact that it is not an easy environment in which to be open. Those who do write of the rural lesbian speak of the utter isolation experienced when one is surrounded by an ultra-conservative, family-oriented community. Where little or no anonymity exists, one fears harassment, ostracism, and possible violence if one is discovered. Belitsos (1983) and Breeze (1981) address the issue of the paranoia of lesbian youth who tend to be all the more visible in a rural setting. Deprived of role models, they often internalize and mimic the image of negatives stereotypes seen in the media. The often resulting stereotypical behavior subjects them to additional hostility by parents, general ridicule, and potential physical and/or sexual violence. Many young people, as well as adults, turn to drugs and alcohol; others run away.

Among older lesbians, the fear of discovery may, according to Buckner and Moses (1982), actually cause them to avoid contact with other lesbians, further increasing their isolation. Moreover, socialized as country women, they may be uncomfortable going to a city club to seek out companions.

There is also a sizable lesbian population living in collectives on the land. Since many are separatists, they may seek little or no contact with heterosexual town life. They do, however, have financial concerns and the need to acquire skills which will enable them to live independently off the land. Likewise, there is a need for mediation in communal affairs and for lesbian therapy. Moreover, separatists or not, many collectives remain, by their very location, isolated from other collectives and lesbian communities.

Networking is the means to tie the individual or individual group to others, usually located in larger towns or university towns. Where there is lack of access to city groups, a worker may help coordinate a group made up of local individual lesbians, but one might anticipate trouble identifying or doing outreach to the "hidden" population. In the case of lesbian youth, Breeze (1981) suggests tying them into existing youth services and sensitizing the workers to their special needs and concerns. Belitsos (1983), too, calls for the sensitivity training of police and probation workers. Finally, Breeze urges professionals to come out as lesbians and gays, and from this position of "professional credibility" to advocate for this population and to serve as role models.

Where all other contact or networking is difficult or impossible, there remains the possibility of bridging the isolation through reading. Making contact with a lesbian bookstore and ordering material through catalogs will help to inform, as well as to connect. Moreover, there are publications like *Lesbian Connection* and *Open Door* which, as a cross between a community bulletin board, a directory of contact persons throughout the world, and a newspaper, greatly reduce distances.

Much work is needed in this area. Information is foremost. Research, at best difficult if not impossible because of the fear of identification as lesbians, would help to identify who this population actually is and to delineate their needs. In this way, this population could be better integrated into the lesbian community or into a friendship network. The training of staff and the funding of programs for lesbians in existent mainstream agencies are also in order.

LESBIANS IN PRISON

Little information exists on lesbians in prison. Researchers would agree on the need for advocacy and counseling for this population. They also break this population into two groups: those who engage in lesbian activity out of deprivation and those who continue to live according to a pre-established pattern of lesbianism regardless of whether they are lesbian youth or older lesbians. According to Shakur (1978), a great deal of the behavior of this population reflects the exploitation, violence, and role playing in the oppressive environment. In addition, many women have little or no understanding of lesbianism or feminism. Despite the bleak picture painted of this population, one is reminded of their need for warmth, love, care, and mutual support.

Research could create a clearer image of the needs of lesbians in correctional facilities. Outreach by lesbian organizations, suggested by Jackson (1978), could help inform the population and integrate it into a broader lesbian community. Training for counselors assigned to prison infirmaries or for counselors in correctional facilities for youth could sensitize them to the harassment and violence committed against these women.

OTHER MINORITIES

As a final note, this researcher can only reiterate the theme of certain subtopics within this section on minorities. There is a need for collective action on the part of all "minorities." One must acknowledge the difference that exists between groups and welcome that difference. A call for the visibility or the various sub-groups of the lesbian minority will also bring forth the numbers which will necessitate action for, by, and about lesbians. This action must include research, personal narratives, funding, programs, and political action to effect changes in policies that categorically keep minorities invisible, separate from one another, and therefore ineffective.

III. LESBIAN FAMILIES

FAMILY OF ORIGIN

Having come to a sense of who she is, the lesbian may seek to share her new identity with her family of origin. Then, too, her family may confront her or may have already asked or caused her to disclose her lesbian identity. The growing literature on coming out to parents is usually most supportive of both the parents or the family of origin of the lesbian and of the lesbian herself.

Most writers have focused on the feelings of grief and loss experienced by the family. They grieve the loss of the child they "used" to know, who now, in their eyes, is different and lost to them. They grieve their fantasies for their child: marriage, grandchildren, and so forth. Sauerman (1984) compares this grieving process to the stages of Kubler-Ross. Wirth (1978), too, speaks of denial and anger. Confusion and guilt over responsibility -- over how they, as parents, have failed their daughter -- are other emotions that enter into play soon after the initial disclosure of a daughter's lesbianism. If parents continue to deny or hide their daughter's lesbianism, according to Carlson (1984), they also experience the painful feelings of stigma with which a lesbian fearful of coming out lives. In this early stage, parents need to be assured of their daughter's love (just as she needs to be assured of theirs), to be reassured that they've done nothing to cause this, and to know that they are not alone. They can be encouraged to join with other parents of lesbians (and gays) in groups led by parents, as Ashworth (1981) insists, or facilitated by social workers. Beck (1981), who insists that it is not necessary for parents of gays to lead the groups, describes a six-stage group. This group is comprised of an introductory stage, three stages of disclosure, one of historical perspectives with a review of the literature in an effort to break down myths and stereotypes and a stage of discussion of reaction and feelings followed up by a session with a guest speaker, possibly a member of the clergy. In the final session the children form a circle within the larger circle of the parents. Here, they discuss similar processes of coming out, and the parents are urged to let go of their self-centered loss and to concentrate on the feelings of their children.

Likewise, after the acknowledgment of feelings, Wirth's (1978) stages include contemplation, decision-making, problem-solving, and acceptance. DeVine's (1984) systems approach takes into account the general cohesiveness of the whole family, the regulations and the themes which the family seems to project for the outside

world. In the first two stages of "subliminal awareness" and
then disclosure, parents and family usually experience
denial, guilt, isolation, and anger with potential lowered self-
esteem and depression. There may very well be a fear of
role failure and loss of boundaries. In the third stage,
various coping mechanisms are at work in an effort to regain
the status quo. Following this, one often attempts to
bargain in order to control behavior and to silence the feared
word ("As long as you don't mention the word
'homosexual,' we can act as if you're okay"). The worker's
task is to help bring the family to an understanding that
control will not resolve the issue or integrate the family, to
help clarify interactions within the family, and to help draw
out the feelings whose expression is necessary for the next
step. Here, one begins to resolve the issues, mourning the
loss of roles, rules, and themes. Lesbian-Affirmative
knowledge is necessary to break myths and to confront
stereotypes. It is only after this mourning process that
integration can occur as a life-long possibility of
communication which promotes self-actualization, as well as
the means for the system to reconstruct itself and come to a
full acceptance of the lesbian (or gay) member.

From the viewpoint of the lesbian, there is also great
fear and guilt. She, too, needs to be assured of the
continued love of her parents and continued open
communication. Most writers advise her to come to a
clarification of her feelings before she approaches her
family. To present an unsure, ambivalent attitude, or
especially a negative one, may only incur greater fears or
trivialization on their part. Rather, one can better avoid the
risk of parents' suggesting a "cure," a rest, or a heterosexual
date by being positive in one's approach. Writers further
warn against disclosure at such stressful or highly charged
times as holidays, weddings, or quarrels. One is urged to
disclose only what is adequate and understandable, using
familiar concepts of love, marriage, relationship. Initially

exposing parents to an overabundance of sexual information or gay scenes (bars, community centers) may alienate them at this point. If denial occurs, the subject must be broached again, and parents must be given time to contemplate the disclosure. It is suggested that one can anticipate reactions based on the level of the relationship before disclosure.

Authors also discuss the need to consider the risks of coming out to family. In the case of custody, coming out to one's family or to one's children may cause a reopening or a challenge of custody. A final consideration is the relative advantage or disadvantage of coming out or remaining closeted with one's family. The lesbian is urged to consider what will be accomplished by disclosure and to weigh carefully the possible outcomes.

LESBIAN COUPLES

Most of the research concerning couples centers around the questions of the similarity of lesbian couples to heterosexual couples and autonomy versus merger within lesbian couples.

Peplau (1981) and Peplau, Cochran, Rook, and Padesky (1978) find mostly similarities in the values possessed by lesbian and heterosexual couples. The greatest differences (other than the weight of the stigma attached to lesbianism and lesbian relationships) seem to result from gender difference, not from sexual preference. The values expressed by lesbians, more like those of heterosexual women than men (gay or heterosexual), focus on equality of power, emotional expressiveness, and self-disclosure. Lesbian relationships are characterized by stability, an absence of role playing, and satisfaction. The greater the balance of power of resources and of distancing and intimacy, the greater the satisfaction expressed. Compared to heterosexual women, lesbians seem to favor more sexual openness and a greater similarity of beliefs between the partners. Consistent with these results are Mendola's (1980) findings on the stability of lesbian couples and the general similarities of lesbian and heterosexual couples. Moreover, Shrag (1984) mentions additional positive differences in the greater range of choices and individual freedom in the lesbian couple and better coping skills from having overcome stigma.

Stigma, then, would seem to be the factor that most differentiates lesbian from heterosexual couples. The effects of stigma are multifaceted and work against the couple in no simple way. A total lack of validation of the lesbian couple by society often results in the drawing closer together of the lesbian partners. Likewise, the couple's boundaries are transgressed by old friends and family members who fail to invite the partner to parties and/or family functions or who match the lesbian up with dates. Turning to one another for security against a hostile environment, the partners in a lesbian dyad may accidentally isolate and alienate themselves in an effort to affirm their couple and to protect against the intrusion of the stigmatizing heterosexual world. Most researchers in this study address this issue and hold it accountable for a tendency of the couple to merge. Krestan and Bepko (1980) also refer to a lack of validation of the couple by some lesbian communities, which view monogamy as a mimicking of heterosexual marriage. Likewise, Dilno (1978) and Whitlock (1978) look to the lesbian's socialization in the heterosexual world as the rationale for monogamy and self-effacement. A lack of mourning for this old heterosexual self may also result in one's turning inward towards the couple. This, according to Krestan and Bepko (1980), can also breed hostility within the tightness of the couple.

The issue, then, is the resulting tendency in some couples to bond too closely. Researchers address the need for distancing. Kaufman, Harrison, and Hyde (1984) refer to intimacy as a function of distance. The less isolated from one's environment one is, and the more autonomous one is, the more intimate one can be without hostility over the loss of one's self. According to Sang (1984), lesbians' socialization as women is at the root of this "nurturing" or bonding. Elise (1986) reiterates the view that merger is not so much a "homosexual" issue as it is a gender issue stemming from early separation-individuation dynamics between mother and child.

Separation-individuation theory is likewise examined by Lindenbaum (1985). She sees the two-woman dyad as unconsciously re-creating the primary intimacy between mother and child. The often resulting feeling of loss of self can then trigger a mechanism of sexual distancing, then "pseudo-mutuality" (where the partners attempt to cover up differences between themselves, since, in effect, they share one "self"), and "pseudo-difference" (where a partner attempts to assert her difference from her partner at all costs). Lindenbaum claims that some lesbians experience "envy" during a "felt-difference" stage where an undifferentiated self vies for a "shared quality," the loss of which through a partner's distancing would signify the total loss of it in self. Instead, she says, lesbians must "compete" as separate, autonomous selves for qualities and skills which will allow each of them to grow as individuals. A lack of this "healthy" competition can only lead to a break-up of the couple as the final, inevitable outcome of "pseudo-difference."

In general, Peplau et al. (1978) find feminists more autonomous than non-feminists. These researchers do not, however, see autonomy and dyadic attachments as "polar opposites" and believe that one does not exclude the other.

Their findings, moreover, show that most women who have a high degree of closeness in their relationship experience satisfaction.

Other issues discussed by many researchers are the potential difference in resources due to difference in jobs and the tendency to overlap the lines between friend and lover. Krestan and Bepko (1980) and Sang (1984) address this issue and the possible jealousy, confusion of roles, and potential break-ups as friendship becomes sexual and interferes with a primary relationship, leading to "sexual monogamy." Lynch and Reilly (1986) and Roth (1985) mention sexuality and recognize a source of possible conflict over the initiation of sex, which partner starts it and how often. In addition, Roth relates a few instances of sexual dysfunction based on inconsistencies of desires: one partner wants to cuddle, the other wants more; preferences or dislikes in sex practices; discomfit in sex. Brown (1986) attributes this sexual dysfunction to the internalization of stigma which results in some lesbians' viewing lesbian sexuality as all-perverted or all-ideal.

Another, final issue in this section deals with therapies. Most researchers see a systems approach as the therapy of choice. A "here and now" approach coupled with feminism and ego psychology is also predominant. Researchers call for knowledge of the lesbian community and the various political, cultural, social, and religious groups found there; a tying of the couple into the community; work on distancing; and the building of stronger ego boundaries. Kaufman et al. (1984) discuss assertiveness training, communication skills, and stress management. Shrag (1984) calls for work on potentially different stages of the coming out process and drawing out issues of internalization of stigma. He, moreover, urges the worker to get in touch with the lesbian community to educate himself or herself, to develop good group skills, and to use a systems approach. Additionally, he stresses the importance of a heterosexual therapist's resolving his/her own feelings in relation to lesbianism and homosexuality.

FAMILY OF PROCREATION

The Lesbian as Mother

Researchers speak of a new type of family: the lesbian couple and children, in which children come from former marriages or are born through artificial insemination by donor (AID). Little information from the point of view of the mother or family itself is available since most studies have concentrated on proof of wellness for children of lesbians involved in custody disputes. Yet, the lesbian mother, who is less visible as a lesbian than non-mothers, is the subject of some studies which, in general, affirm her right, her capacity, and her choice to be a mother. Among others, Hanscombe (1982) finds no difference in her mothering ability as compared with heterosexual mothers and concludes that motherhood is motherhood regardless of sexual preference. Saphira (1984) affirms the positive experience of motherhood for the lesbian, a position which is upheld by Beck (1983), who speaks of motherhood in terms of one's choice, open to all women, lesbian or non-lesbian. This affirmation comes in the context of the difficult position of the lesbian mother, rejected by heterosexuals and some factions of the lesbian community. Steinhorn (1982) and Beck (1983) address the issue of the false myths of the "monster mother," believed guilty of incest and perversion. Likewise, some lesbians, according to Beck, question the lesbian's desire to be a mother.

Another aspect of the research focuses on guilt and social stigma. While most studies find no difference in mothering ability, they do mention the lesbian mother's guilt over her choice of lesbianism. Goodman (1977) stresses that this guilt can be worked through, and more easily so when lesbian professionals come out as lesbian mothers. Yet, fear due to social stigma is prevalent. Steinhorn (1982) and Berzon (1978), too, discuss the question of fear: fear of being discovered as a lesbian and the resultant possibility of losing one's job, one's ethnic or religious group, and ultimately one's child through a custody dispute.

Advantages, though, stem from one's having overcome this stigma. Lesbian mothers become more self-reliant and realize an increase in coping skills. Goldstein (1986), Lorde (1984), and Steinhorn (1982) refer to the lesbian mother who, having dealt successfully with intolerance, communicates her resiliency to her children. This mother is more likely to foster tolerance for difference of every kind and self-actualization in her own child, male or female.

The Lesbian and Childbirth

Because of the difficulty in maintaining custody and because of the choice of some lesbians to parent, many lesbians are considering alternative means of parenting. Study in this field is concentrated on artificial insemination by donor (AID) and the new legal issues arising from this choice. AID, however, is only one option, and several of the works describe the possibility of foster care and adoption. Pies (1985) includes exercises to enable the future mothers and co-mothers (her partner in the relationship or family) to decide if parenting, and which form of it, is appropriate for them. Goldstein (1986) describes the greater stability now experienced by gay couples and their desire, therefore, to better fit into society as parents. Hanscombe (1982) also addresses the issue of lesbians taking charge of their own conception because of the discrimination they face in the medical world. She cites cases of doctors refusing to perform AID with lesbians. Many of the new works, then, enable the lesbian to start the process of finding a donor and deciding on the conditions and implications, legal and other, involved in AID.

Legal issues are another main focus of work in this area. Hitchens' (1984) work on contracts and agreements, as well as the models of legal agreements included in Pies' (1985) work, facilitate dealing with the legalities of artificial insemination. Hitchens specifically mentions the limitation of fathering rights and the inclusion of the rights of the lover of the biological mother in a nomination of guardianship. Wolf (1984), too, calls for the inclusion of the mother's lover from the very beginning of the process. In general, as Goldstein (1986) demonstrates, the concerns of lesbians (and gays) involved in parenting are becoming more concrete. General rights, insurance coverage, and medical benefits are of utmost importance; along with the fight for easier access to AID and other means of parenting, one has to fight for the rights which will render the gay family its security and its due.

Although there is a growing literature on lesbian (and gay) parenting, more legal information is necessary, as well as studies showing the impact of AID on children procreated by means of it. In general, there is a paucity of studies on the lesbian couple, of longevity factors, and of changing attitudes reflective of the atmosphere of the mid-1980s. As of September 1986, there are calls for articles and materials for three works on lesbian couples. To date, these works would seem to be general anthologies of couples' personal narratives from which, just the same, more information will happily be gleaned. One hopes that more studies on lesbian mothers will be undertaken, specifically from the point of view of the mother, as well as of the co-mother where she exists.

IV.   OPPRESSION

HETEROSEXISM IN THEORY

Oppression of lesbians has been addressed by many writers who label it homophobia. Homophobia (an exaggerated fear of same-sex attraction in oneself and in others) is culture-bound according to Gramick (1983). Because of a fear of one's potential "conversion" to homosexuality, the heterosexual directs his/her hostility outward onto homosexuals, who are pictured as deviants capable of destroying family life. Gramick examines the example of North African Moslem society where homosexuality (among men) is tolerated. Despite this, family life flourishes there.

However, homophobia as oppression of lesbians is perhaps more adequately examined under the title of heterosexism. Lesbian theorists Rich (1984) and Bunch (cited in Arnup, 1983) define this as the institutionalized assumption that every woman wants to be bonded economically and emotionally to a man. Accordingly, everyone and everything is heterosexual, and heterosexuality is a preference. Rich and Bunch claim that, in fact, heterosexism offers no preference at all. Rich (1984) speaks of it as an "unquestioned acquiescence to patriarchal privilege" (p. 139). She says that in order to protect this

privilege, society believes it is imperative to silence
lesbianism, to cloud it in taboos and labels of deviance.
Because of the overwhelming power of woman-bonding and
the power of women's spirituality, men fear being displaced
by this power. Hence, lesbianism is outlawed, and in order
to prevent women from seeing through this form of social
control of woman's power, they are given the illusion of
preference for men. In truth, there is no choice.

Since heterosexism insures patriarchal privilege
which governs the capitalist system, it is, according to Rich
(1984), the root of all exploitation and illegitimate control.
The roots of racism, sexism, and classism are contained
within it.   Goodman (1980), too, speaks of this
institutionalized homophobia and traces the origin of racism,
sexism, and classism to the same source.   Just as Rich
(1984) claims that all women will profit from fighting
heterosexism, even if they choose men, so, too, Goodman
(1978) calls for all people to root out this oppressive script in
an effort to tolerate difference and imperfection among all
people.   Moreover, she examines imperfection and
difference among heterosexuals and asks one to assume and
accept that same difference and imperfection among
homosexuals.

Attitudes towards lesbians have been viewed
differently over the years. Bayer (1981) and Conrad and
Schneider (1980) describe the evolution of homosexual
stigma from one of sin to crime to disease.   Since the
removal in 1973 of homosexuality from the *Diagnostic and
Statistical Manual of Mental Disorders (DSM)*, Conrad and
Schneider (1980) see the stigma attached to homosexuality
as returning to a moral or criminal model, and in a
controversial vein, these authors hypothesize that
homosexuals are more vulnerable now that they have been
divested of the limited protection that the label "sickness"
accords (p. 213). Herek (1984), too, refers to the different

types of rationales for the oppressive attitudes against homosexuality. He speaks of these attitudes as experiential, based on actual exposure to gays; symbolic, based on one's values; and defensive, based on one's own self-image and identity role. Identifying which one is at play can facilitate the modification or change of that attitude. Likewise, Hardesty (1981) examines biblical references to homosexuality and shows, through a change in interpretation, that these citations are, in truth, innocuous to homosexuality.

The outward expression of negative attitudes toward homosexuality, which is homophobia, often extends beyond the assumption of heterosexuality or stigmatized labeling of "deviants." Too often, violence against gays is the result. Norman (1981) refers to the rape and brutalization of lesbians. DeCrescenzo (1985) examines the mental violence that has been committed by health professionals against lesbians (and gays) and finds social workers in her poll to be among the most homophobic (p. 130). Moreover, there is an abundance of stories about therapists who try to bolster their own heterosexuality by attempting to seduce or convert homosexuals.

HETEROSEXISM IN PRACTICE

In the Courts - Custody

Patriarchal privilege is likewise under attack in the courts. The existence of lesbianism shows the patriarchal system to be less than perfect. In addition, the lesbian dares, as an unfit woman, to challenge her ex-husband's custodial rights. Thus, according to Hunter and Polikoff (1979), the denial of custody is partriarchy's way of punishing the lesbian.

Judges in custody cases are supposedly considering "the best interests of the child"; they will, in fact, examine the sole issue of the lesbianism of the mother. Most cases result in a denial of custodial rights to lesbians and/or severe limitations to visitation rights: the mother's lover may not be present, the child may not spend the night, and so forth. Judges claim that in the long run the mother's lesbianism is detrimental to the child; most rule in favor of the father or even for placement in a juvenile institution, despite the testimony of expert witnesses. There is only one instance, the case of Hatzapoulous (*Re Hatzapoulous*, 1977), where custody is actually granted to the lover of the deceased mother.

In an effort to demonstrate the best interests of the child, most researchers focus their studies on the emotional and psychological well-being of the child, the mothering he/she receives, and the development of gender and sex roles. Researchers consistently find that there is no significant difference in the overall emotional and psychological well-being of the children of lesbians as compared with those of heterosexual mothers. Green (1982), Green, Mandel, Hotvedt, Gray and Smith (1986), and Kleber, Howell, and Tibbits-Kleber (1986) urge one to look at the quality of the relationship between the child and the mother and at her ability to foster growth in the child, not at the sexual preference of the mother. Concerning this relationship, Lewis (1980) finds that although the children of lesbians express some ambivalence towards their mothers, they are proud of her standing up and challenging society's rules. Likewise, more than 71 percent of the children in the study of Harris and Turner (1986) are either indifferent to or supportive of their mother's choice. Moreover, Nungesser (1980) claims that the children recognize that society's negative attitudes need to be changed.

Concerning conflict over sexual identity, researchers report no confusion in the children. Nungesser's (1980) study of sex role acquisition focuses on the potential modeling of the androgynous characteristics of the lesbian mother. No conclusions concerning direct modeling are forthcoming, and accordingly, even if studies are to be made, researchers will have to examine closely if and how lesbian mothers would or could reinforce this modeling behavior. The mother's "androgyny" is characterized by self-assertiveness, independence, an ability to stand up for rights, leadership, and ambition. Authors agree that the children of lesbians may, in fact, be more flexible, independent, and aware of greater options in life. According to Golombok, Spencer, and Rutter (1983), they are also more likely to have support, nurturing, and companionship because of the more likely presence of the mother's lover in the house, as opposed to the less frequent presence of a male lover in the household of a divorced heterosexual mother. Moreover, most researchers indicate that, concerning gender and sexual identity, children are influenced by the total environment, not solely by their mothers (Rees, 1979). Likewise, they are more influenced by their peers and television (Hoeffer, 1981).

In a final note concerning differences in the children of lesbians, there is a potential negative impact on children if the mother has not adjusted well to her lesbianism. In the study of Rand, Graham, and Rawlings (1982), the lesbian mother is seen to be the happiest when she is open about her lesbianism. This, then, would help to insure her psychological well-being and that of her children. Ironically, it is just this openness with which judges take issue, demanding most often that the lesbian mother avoid all publicity and all mention of her lesbianism.

These findings have, for the most part, not dissuaded judges from ruling against custody for the lesbian mother.

What remains to be done for the lesbian mother, and why are custody disputes so controversial for feminist activists and lawyers alike? According to Hunter and Policoff (1979) and Hitchens (1981), the major obstacle in custody law is the wide discretion over rulings with which judges are empowered and the lack of precedence-setting. One successful case only serves to satisfy the immediate needs of the family and to educate or raise the consciousness of others. A successful case will not set a precedent. Fund-raising to cover the legal costs is a difficult issue since the use of the lesbian mother's name would incur publicity against which judges have issued warning. Several groups, such as Wages Due Lesbians, are leading fund-raising campaigns that manage to maintain the anonymity of the mother.

In general, one is urged to try to settle out of court. If this is not possible, procuring a sympathetic lawyer experienced with this type of case is the next step. The mother must then decide what she is willing to: remain closeted, live without her lover, or avoid publicity. The use of legal and health professionals as expert witnesses is also advisable. Finally, the hope is that education, the breaking of myths, and wider sensitization to the issue will foster more rulings in favor of the mother.

In the Workplace

Another domain of male privilege is the workplace. Once again, lesbians are discriminated against as women and as lesbians. Valeska (1981), refers to the classic case of the woman who resists sexual overtures. She is immediately suspected of not being interested in sex, and in effect, of being a lesbian. Harassment often ensues, with possible ostracism by peers and superiors, and, more often, with an overzealous and scrupulous supervision of her work.

Discrimination on the job may be actual or anticipated. Studies (National Gay Task Force, 1981, Levine and Leonard, 1984, Shachar and Gilbert, 1983, Schneider 1984) indicate that between 21 and 24 percent of the respondents actually are discriminated against, whereas more than 60 percent anticipate being fired, not employed, or passed over for promotion if their lesbianism is discovered. Concerning federal and state policy for employees, Hedgpeth (1979) sums up the trend as being one of finding the nexus. One must prove the connection between the homosexual behavior and the inability to do the work in order to dismiss or uphold the dismissal of a lesbian (or gay). Yet, Eversley (1981) relates the story of her own dismissal from the Louisiana State Bureau for Women because she disclosed her lesbianism at a staff meeting.

In the private sector, where no nondiscrimination policy exists or in the absence of a city or state nondiscrimination ordinance, the employer has wide discretion, and, in any event, would probably veil the true reason for firing the lesbian.

In addition to the overt discrimination against the woman whose lesbianism is known or suspected, the lesbian herself experiences intrarole conflict as lowered self-esteem. The lesbian's mechanism to cope with the conflict of being out or closeted on the job usually amounts to denial or avoidance. According to Shachar and Gilbert (1983), the environment controls the lesbian's choice of strategy. The end result is that she is, in effect, powerless to retain her job if she asserts her lesbian identity. Thus, she may retain her job, but at a high cost to her self-esteem.

This conflict is all the more significant for lesbians since most lesbians, responsible for their own economic survival, must work. In addition, according to Schneider

(1984), many lesbians have a tendency to integrate work and social life because of the difficulty of other social outlets. This causes anxiety, especially in professional women who are expected to socialize with colleagues, but who risk all the more by being discovered.

The need for legislation, according to Valeska (1981) and the National Gay Task Force (1981), is twofold. Corporations must effect nondiscrimination policies and publicize them so employees are aware of their rights and less stressed as a result. Furthermore, municipal and state ordinances must be passed top guarantee basic civil rights. The NGTF (1981) study shows that the mere existence of a company policy does not suffice to assure a relaxing of the conflict experienced by gays. They need to be aware that their rights to the job are also insured by the city or state.

General Civil Rights

Concerning the rights issue in general, one thing is immediately obvious: there are very few titles contained in this study that pertain directly to lesbian (and gay) rights. This is consistent with the actual state of basic civil rights for lesbians (and gays.) The general consensus of all writers on this topic is that in the absence of "guarantees of freedom," one must use the law. One must draw up the wills, the powers of attorney, the contracts which spell out the conditions under which gays live and share their goods, and name the names of their lovers, their benefactors, their visitors in hospital, and their co-decision makers in matters of life and death. Where the law may be too patriarchal, one may use mediators within the lesbian community (Schneider, 1984).

In the absence of ordinances in all but 55 American cities, lesbians must risk being visible. This visibility proves to the legislators and to the financial establishment that gays exist in great numbers (more than 10 percent of the population), numbers which vote and consume. Gays do make a difference. Gay advocacy groups exist, as do lesbian and gay lawyers and gay fund-raising. In February 1986, gays in New York City won a long-awaited struggle: the passage of the gay rights bill. In June 1986, the patriarchal system retaliated with two sounding blows: the Supreme Court decision in *Bowers vs. Hardwick* (1986) to uphold the right of the state of Georgia to enforce sodomy laws between two consenting adults and the recommendation of the Department of Justice to allow employers to fire employees with AIDS out of "fear of contamination."

The section on rights in this study is all but nonexistent. Advocacy, legislative action in the form of lobbying and constituency visibility, and fund-raising are necessary. In the aftermath of the Supreme Court decision, the gay riots and demonstrations are perhaps a sign that more information and action are forthcoming. What remains obvious is the need for education of all people, a consciousness-raising by means of studies of lesbians, as mothers, as workers, as consumers, and as voters. These studies should then be made available to employers, legislators, bankers, the medical establishment, and so forth since an estimated 19 percent or more of their employees, constituents, customers, etc. are gay. Further, they need to be reminded that a people, disempowered by discrimination and abuse, cannot work effectively; yet, an angry, frustrated people still has the power to vote office holders in or out, to shop one place or another, to name itself and its needs, hence, to act according to its values.

V.   HEALTH

GENERAL & GYNECOLOGICAL

The health field and, in particular, gynecological medicine present several difficult issues for the lesbian. Here, the assumption of heterosexuality combined with sexism and homophobia interact to make gynecological treatment a potentially threatening experience for the lesbian. Because of the assumption of heterosexuality, gynecology is geared to the heterosexual woman and, therefore, to reproduction or contraception. Women who do not ask for contraception (or who are not using any), are treated as if they are ignorant. Or, they may be blamed for being a potential burden on society should they become pregnant. The assumption is that in order to be a healthy, sexual being, one must be having "safe" sex with a man or trying to become pregnant. Should a physician discover the woman's lesbianism, treatment may be adversely affected. In addition, discrimination in the health area includes lack of visitation rights for a lover in intensive care units, lack of medical insurance coverage for the lover, and lack of decision-making capacity for the lover in a life or death situation.

Authors agree that practitioners must make themselves aware of the patient's psychosocial sexual history. By formulating questions carefully (for example, after asking, "How often do you have sex?" adding, "with both sexes or just the opposite?"), the practitioner demonstrates that he/she is supportive of either choice of sexual behavior. Brossart (1979) says that to leave the burden of volunteering information on a fearful patient is a potentially dangerous situation. Diagnoses may be delayed or falsely made based on insufficient information or an assumption of heterosexuality. Brossart cites the example of the lesbian admitted to the emergency room with severe abdominal pain. According to Brossart, if the practitioner had known she was a lesbian, he/she could have immediately eliminated pregnancy and concentrated on the potentially ruptured appendix.

Another condition which is virtually nonexistent among lesbians is venereal disease. Vaginal infection and cervical cancer are likewise evidenced less frequently among lesbians. The potential contraction of an infection transmitted through the bowel is common to all, lesbian and heterosexual, who practice anal sex. The lesbian who has not had a child, however, is among those women who run a higher risk of breast cancer and endometriosis (O'Donnell, 1978; O'Donnell, Pollock, Leoffler, and Saunders, 1979; Robertson and Shachter, 1981).

Several recommendations concerning improvement of service delivery to the lesbian have been consistent. The need for disclosure on the part of the lesbian and for discreet information-seeking on the part of the practitioner is foremost, as well as an examination of one's thinking on lesbians and lesbianism and its potential impact on one's provision of care. Johnson and Palermo (1984) suggest that a friend or social worker accompany a lesbian to the gynecologist's office to advocate for her, as well as to offer her support. In addition to the establishment of women-run clinics with at last one lesbian on staff and the formation of illness support groups, Darty and Potter (1984), O'Donnell (1978), and O'Donnell et al. (1979) call for wider research on and study of the special health needs of lesbians. Little is known on this topic and still less is taught in medical schools.

MENTAL HEALTH

Alcoholism

A major health concern of lesbians is alcoholism and alcohol. There is much debate as to what exactly constitutes alcoholism and why alcohol affects some populations and individuals more adversely than others; however, researchers agree that the consumption of alcohol among lesbians is significantly higher than among heterosexuals and that there must be a change in the drinking behavior within the lesbian community.

A depressant, alcohol has a sedative effect which allows a person to neutralize his/her inability to deal with internal or external conflict (Taylor, 1982a, p. 7). Continuing with this description of alcohol, Taylor (1982b) calls alcohol the symptom and claims the disease is homophobia, producing alcohol abuse, lowered self-esteem, depression, chronic stress, compulsive behavior, and suicide (p. 2). Ziebold and Mongeon (1982) call alcoholism an addictive behavior for relieving anxiety and paranoia and predict its incidence based on the ratio of organic factors and stress to competence, self-esteem, and support groups (p. 92). Again, in creating an illusion of safety, alcohol, according to Nardi (1982a), is a denial mechanism and alienates one from one's feelings.

Whether one conceptualizes homophobia as the disease, one must grapple with the high percentage of lesbians affected by problem drinking. Fifield (cited in Anderson and Henderson, 1985), Weathers (1981), Lewis, Saghir, and Robins (1982), and Zehner and Lewis (1985) consistently find that between 30 and 35 percent of the lesbian community is troubled by alcohol abuse. From the definitions given above, one already images an individual with lowered self-esteem experiencing conflict, anxiety and/or paranoia, and spiritual and possibly social alienation. According to Taylor (1982a) and Nardi (1982a), the individual's sense of trust is the security of the alcohol. One delineates the portrait in greater detail when, along with Fifield (cited in Anderson and Henderson, 1985), Nardi (1982a), Taylor (1982a, 1982b), Weathers (1981), and Ziebold and Mongeon (1982), one views the lesbian as a member of a stigmatized minority and as a woman. The lesbian has had to cope with her family's and society's denial of lesbianism or its portrayal of lesbianism as deviant and sinful. She has had to pretend her feelings for women didn't exist, or deny, or adapt to the stereotype of the isolated, role-playing deviant who could only find acceptance in lesbian bars. She has learned to pretend everything's all right, denying over a long period of time that she lives with stigma and alienation. This, in turn, leads to a tendency to seek instant gratification or relief.

As a woman, her self-esteem suffers in a sexist society which traditionally offers her limited options and binds her to self-effacing roles. Taylor (1982b) mentions Broverman's study in which the discrepancy between the characteristics of a healthy male and those of a healthy female leave one to wonder if a woman can ever be healthy in a sexist environment. Although the lesbian is less tied to rigid roles, and therefore, according to Taylor, more likely to be considered along the lines of a healthy male, she has no healthy homosexual model to look for (p. 6). Concerning characteristics of well-adjusted individuals, Ziebold and Mongeon (1982) cite Glenn's study, which finds individuals at high risk for chemical dependency to be deficient in one or more of these characteristics: identification with a viable role model, identification with responsibility for family processes, low faith in miracle solutions to problems, adequate inter- and intra- personal skills, skills for dealing with systems, and judgment skills. They view the gay person as being at greater risk since he/she experiences "trouble with competence and coping skills while confronting isolation and separation from family, institutions, and people responsible for instilling those skills" (p. 93).

The means of bridging the isolation and combatting stigma would seem to be activity in the lesbian community. Yet, "membership" in some bar-oriented communities is another factor which contributes to the high incidence of alcohol abuse among lesbians. Taylor (1982a), Weathers (1981), and Ziebold and Mongeon (1982) hold that because of the centrality of the lesbian bar within the lesbian community, it is most difficult to avoid alcohol consumption in the lesbian world. Meeting place, hub of political activity, and refuge for some, the bar is perhaps the most accessible lesbian institution, especially for the woman new to the lesbian world. Moreover, in an effort to protect the lesbian from further stigmatization, the community itself often denies its alcoholism. The community, too, attempts to cope with the stigmatization it has endured over the years. Further, compared to heterosexual society, there has been a lack of resources to address the problem of alcoholism within the community and to create and fund programs.

The role of the co-alcoholic, the person who "intervenes in such a way as to prevent the alcoholic from facing the consequences of his/her actions" (Whitney, cited in Anderson and Henderson, 1985, p. 522), is perhaps more significant in a lesbian relationship. Given the lack of validation of the lesbian couple by society, and the tendency, therefore, to affirm one's couple by bonding more closely against a homophobic society, the impact of the alcoholism on the couple may entail feelings of increased fears, anger, powerlessness, and possibly, physical abuse. With alcoholism there ensures a shift in the balance of power. Fenwick (1978) and Nardi (1982b) suggest that where a couple had shared an egalitarian relationship, now the lover of the alcoholic becomes the enabler, the one in control. She may cling to this role and, thus, help perpetuate the alcoholism. If the alcoholic stops drinking, the co-alcoholic stands to lose power and possibly her lover, once the dependency need no longer exists.

This bleak picture of the increased vulnerability of some lesbians to alcoholism, clarifies the need, according to Snyder (cited in Ziebold and Mongeon, 1982), for increasing the resistance to alcohol and decreasing the adverse characteristics of the urban gay environment. The general goals of treatment are to prevent denial and to foster self-esteem. According to Diamond and Wilsnack (1978), self-esteem is fostered through a heightened sense of effectiveness and power. The ultimate goal is to enable responsible determination of one's own values, role, and behavior, including one's drinking. Researchers agree that treatment must focus immediately on sobriety and concomitantly on a restructuring of one's leisure time. Treatment groups address denial, stigma, and alienation and function as support networks for assertiveness training, values clarification, stress management, communications, creativity, and relationship skills.

According to Driscoll (1982), Marcelina (1979), Taylor (1982b), and Ziebold and Mongeon (1982), since the community is the general arena of support and recreational and social life, changes must carry over to the community. The community is called upon to offer alcohol-free space, that is, a safe environment in which one may stop the active drinking stage, and further alcohol-free re-entry programs whereby drinking is not the behavior necessary to socialize with one's old and new friends. In general, the community must learn to alter its norms, its pattern of denial of alcoholism and of stigma and, according to Taylor (1982b), show how alcohol actually impedes the use of the community network. According to Driscoll (1982), the community must educate its leaders in alcohol prevention and volunteer to train staff in alcohol treatment centers on gay and lesbian issues. In the role of public advocacy, community-based action can use a sense of group identity to combat the stigma that renders one susceptible to abuse. Likewise, utilization of community resources serves to confront and combat denial on the part of the community and society through visibility. According to Taylor (1982b), in assuming an activist stance, the alcoholic lends her services to the community thereby gaining new leadership skills and credibility as a role model. Ziebold and Mongeon (1982) claim that additional alcohol-free role models can help to set standards in the community. Campaigns can be organized with bartenders and other leaders to set aside space and time as alcohol-free within the bar and to offer non-alcoholic drinks at reasonable prices. Thus, one can help bring about a shift in the norms of the community, alternative socializing activities, and ultimately a supportive community which recognizes its drinking problem and its responsibility in effecting change.

Several writers also mention the support of Alcoholics Anonymous. Others take issue with the rigidity, conformity, and puritanical attitudes experienced there. Bittle (1982) says that the fault lies rather with some overzealous older members and that the basic "12 Steps" allow for flexibility. He suggests finding a gay sponsor or one who is familiar with the new member's homosexuality. Moreover, there are AA groups especially for lesbians (and gays).

Most of the literature reviewed above is reflective of the attitudes and trends of the early 1980s with more services and information being made available in 1985. Blatantly missing are updated studies on drinking habits and demographics reflective of the increased variety of social institutions within the lesbian community and empirical studies testing the hypothetical predisposition to alcoholism of members of the lesbian community, as well as sources of information on drug abuse. Use among gay men has been acknowledged; yet, the silence concerning its existence within the lesbian community is striking. If such a lesbian community as described above is, at once, susceptible to conflict, minority stress, and compulsive behavior in the form of immediate gratification in order to alleviate this anxiety, and, at the same time, possibly surrounded by the negative support a "user" community can offer, how vulnerable is it to the allure of crack? Or of the wealthy population of professionals, what is known of its use of cocaine and who is treating the abuse? Studies to identify this problem and to involve the community in a campaign of awareness and struggle for a drug-free atmosphere are also needed research projects.

Counseling and Therapy

Many of the studies dealing with lesbians and mental health focus on the distrust of mental health professionals by lesbians who have traditionally been labeled as deviant, neurotic, or in need of being "cured." This attitude has been shown to exist despite the removal in 1973 of homosexuality from the *Diagnostic and Statostical Manual of Mental Disorders*. Some studies demonstrate the positive mental health of the lesbian, while others find her more well-adjusted than the heterosexual woman. Most researchers and mental health professionals supportive of the lesbian agree upon the need for counselors to examine their own feelings toward lesbianism, for staff to be educated and trained as to the needs of lesbians, and for the disclosure of lesbians and gays in the field to act as role models.

Despite the current acceptance (by many, but certainly not all) of the general well-being of the lesbian as a minority dealing with stigma and alienation, she is seen as being more vulnerable than her heterosexual counterpart to certain types of difficulties. The area of major difficulty involves coming out, self-identification, and self-image. This is reflective of the very magnitude of the stress involved in coping with a hostile society which denies or distorts the image of the lesbian. Riddle and Sang (1978) place great emphasis on the lesbian's socialization as a woman and, therefore, also view her as having been traditionally undervalued and disempowered. Some therapists also mention a potential for problems of autonomy and merger in couples and the lack of spontaneity (Sang, 1977) as a result of constantly filtering the expression of feelings. In addition, therapists and theorists discuss the need for special bereavement and breaking-up groups.

A newly exposed need is that of counseling for battered lesbians and lesbian batterers (Lobel, 1986). In an effort to end the denial and silence on the part of individual lesbians and the lesbian community, battered lesbians, lesbian shelter workers, and counselors have begun to speak out. The lesbian world of feminism, nonviolence, and new models for egalitarian relationships cannot claim to provide safe space for all of its members if, out of fear of homophobia and further stigmatization, it denies that this problem of battering exists. Breaking through this wall of silence, lesbians are establishing shelters, groups, and training programs for staff in (heterosexual) battered-women's shelters. Battering as an issue of violence and control, is not inherent to the world of the lesbian, but rather, is reflective of the problem in the macro-society.

The issue of therapy for identity crisis and for self-actualization is perhaps best covered by Woodman and Lenna (1980). Although not every client is in the throes of an identity crisis or in the process of coming out, many clients are in need of work in this area. Woodman and Lenna (1980) discuss their five stages of crisis as a procedure of mourning the loss of the former self, of self-esteem, of former coping patterns, and of support. The first two stages include denial and repression, where the client has to confront the homosexuality, and identity confusion, where the client seeks validation of his/her gayness by the therapist. At this stage, the client expresses anger at other gays whom he/she punishes for being reflective of the negative stereotype which he/she has internalized. The therapist's job is to help the client redirect the anger to the oppression imposed by society and to help tie the client in with positive role models. The next stage involves bargaining on the part of the client to attempt to force the therapist to be the arbiter of the conflict, to accept the responsibility for the situation and to declare the client powerless and the situation hopeless. Anger at the therapist must be redirected at the systems which function as disapproving authority figures. The client's expressing his/her feelings of expectations from authority and/or of the actual power they do or do not weld can immediately help to fit things into perspective and quell anxiety at this stage. If the internalization of the negative stereotype has remained for a long period of time, the client may turn the anger inward. His/her ability to deal with the conflict may translate into a feeling of powerlessness in general. This stage is characteristic of (here) situational depression where the total confusion and cultural dissonance over one's homosexuality is complicated by a lack of external support and a generally weakened sense of self incapable of coping with the inner and outer conflict. Self-definition entails work in expressing feelings, garnering support, goal setting, and problem solving. The client defines gayness according to what he/she thinks it is, wants it to mean, and what he/she has to do in order to achieve this gayness. Sentiment clarification involves the description of one's feelings as what they have been or can be, ought to be, and what one desires them to be. Once the client has discussed this, he/she can realistically view his/her goals and the support available to

help in overcoming obstacles to meeting those goals.
Emphasis is placed on the action necessary to enlist the aid
of the support network. Strategies used include scripting,
role playing, and assertiveness training. Therapists may
intervene in the couple systems, and draw from interfacing
outside support resources and sources of information. The
therapist's general role is to assess the ways for increasing
the client's potential for self-actualization and the support
and coping skills available to the client.

Specific Issues in Therapy

Other approaches favored by therapists whose works
are reviewed in this study are systemic and feminist.
Morrison (1984) has adapted Bowen's theories of family
therapy and stresses the reinforcement of the distinction
between the cognitive and the emotional, the refocusing of
tensions, and a rethinking of undifferentiated ego-syntonic
behavior. Hers is a thinking process involving problem
solving of one's own behavior and task reassignment.
Thus, one works toward new relationships within the family
or couple.

Also proponents of a systems approach, Roth and
Murphy (1986) describe in great detail the circular method of
hypothesis formation based on knowledge of the client's
social contexts, questioning to test hypotheses, modification
of hypotheses, and retesting to arrive at working
hypotheses. These hypotheses describe the client's beliefs
and behaviors in ways that might stimulate change in them.
Roth and Murphy progress from the individual, to the
couple, to the family, to the community contexts, and then to
the context of reciprocally related contests. The circular
hypotheses formulated from the linkage of these multiple
contests are the bases for intervention aimed at enabling the
family to alter self-images and to find new ways of

interacting. According to Roth and Murphy, most of the clients indicate difficulties in relationships with a lover and/or family complicated by identity management.

In a similar fashion, Rothberg and Ubell (1985) employ a systems approach, but one which reflects feminist theory and technique. Incorporating that which is "valid" in each and not offensive to their feminist perspective, they admit that at times feminism must be placed on hold in favor of a systems approach. However, treatment must remain supportive of woman's position and her struggle for equality and self-expression. They hold that role flexibility is a prerequisite for change, that is, in order to bring about new behavior in a system. While they agree that not all lesbians, and moreover, not all of their heterosexual clients, are feminists, they believe that a feminist approach serves to liberate one more fully from the destructive and unnecessary limitations placed on women and, in general, is much more egalitarian. Most of the problems that characterize their lesbian clients are difficulties with families of origin, identity management, autonomy and merger, and power imbalances over resources in couples. In lesbian reconstituted families, strain is sometimes seen between the children and the new lover for whom a role model as co-parent is lacking.

A conclusion one may draw from the works in this section is the need for more lesbian therapists to come out and publish information on their practices. Lesbian therapists acting as role models could, from their position of credibility, help to underscore the need for more and better mental health services for the lesbian community and to inform other health professionals as to the needs of the lesbian community. In addition, research reflective of the changing times and the increase in lesbian visibility, serving as it does to destigmatize the "lesbian" issue, may indicate the lessening of cultural dissonance. As a result, it may also show a reduction of general conflict for the lesbian, as well

as a strengthened lesbian position in the fight for rights and
policy change. These last two may more than likely presage
an increase in the general well-being of the lesbian and the
disempowerment of an oppressive system.

BEYOND THE FINDINGS

Throughout the findings, a theme of difference within sameness has been interwoven. Whether a question of the variety of lifestyles among lesbians who emerge from a variety of classes, races, religions, and ethnic groups, or of different individual "personhoods" within a commonality of lesbian identity or vice versa, or of variance in family codes, rules, and values, the question remains one of difference and similarity. One can make an assumption of heterosexuality and see no difference. So, too, one can make an assumption of homosexuality and see nothing but difference. Moreover, one can visualize no gradation within that difference. All lesbians are different from non-lesbians; therefore, all lesbians are assumed to be the same.

Not merely a matter of semantics, the argument for difference or sameness is a highly politicized trap into which fall a whole gamut of friends and foes, lesbian and heterosexual alike. The issue at hand amounts to nothing less than a whole history of asking, "Is there a difference?" The question has assumed many forms: Are lesbians genetically, physically, or emotionally different? Are they as well, as balanced as heterosexual women? Are they as nurturing as mothers, as loving as daughters? Are they as honorable and as moral as heterosexual teachers and physicians? Many theorists, researchers, scholars and mental health professionals, as well as lesbians not involved in this work, nod in approval at the finding - "no significant difference."

71

Is there, in fact, an argument? And what precisely is at issue when one claims difference or similarity? By asserting similarity, have people bought into social control or "normalized" in a positive way the "lesbian condition"? Likewise, does the label of difference ostracize and perpetuate isolation and cover-ups or cast the lesbian in a visible perspective, differentiated, autonomous, and centered in her demands for recognition and rights?

This chapter, with its treatment of the questions above, targets the professional who interacts with lesbians. In brief, it will focus on who the lesbian is and what the issues of lesbianism are within a context of an oppressive social system system. Conclusions will treat suggestions for current practice, as well as for future work and social change. The general aim is to introduce the professional to the world of the lesbian and to invite this professional to interact with the information in a way as to benefit both the worker and the lesbian client. This aim will have been achieved by this presentation of a positive, insightful image of the lesbian if it creates an instilling of empathy for her, an augmentation of practical skills in order to foster growth and self-actualization in the lesbian, and a desire to advocate publicly for her and expand and ameliorate services for the lesbian.

The initial proponents of the label of difference were clergy, legislators, and doctors. This notion of difference assumed deviance. When these men mentioned lesbians at all, it was to speak of them as sinners, criminals, or mentally ill. The image of the lesbian as an abject aberration of nature was, according to these men, enough of a taboo to deter any other women from even thinking about her. For all practical purposes (maintaining male privilege), this lesbian did not exist. By casting her as different, these men cast her out and denied her.

In retaliation, there has been a great effort to remove this label. After numerous etiological studies, the experts declared that they could not prove what made the lesbian different and that, therefore, she had no scientifically diagnosable sickness or deviance. Abetted by the work of the Mattachine Society, the Daughters of Bilitis, the Gay Liberation Front and the Gay Activist Alliance, professionals who sympathized with the cause helped to have homosexuality removed from the *Diagnostic and Statistical Manual of Mental Disorders (DSM)* in 1973. Lesbians could now be "acceptable." The trend, therefore, was to gratefully accept the new-found "acceptability." To overcome stigma, one set out in study after study to show that no appreciable difference existed between the homosexual and the heterosexual outside of the choice of sex partner. Lesbians fought the stereotype of themselves as monsters, child molesters, and seductresses. Often, they asserted their general similarity to heterosexual women. However, somehow, now unaccountably so, they were predetermined from an early age to be sexually attracted to other women.

As of 1973, the lesbian has been accorded the status of not being deviant or sick and of being basically similar to a heterosexual woman. Has this truly benefitted the lesbian? What actually was achieved? Sociologists Schneider and Conrad (1980) question whether gays really won by the declassification of homosexuality as a sickness. They hold that now gays are once again legally and morally vulnerable. The label of sickness, they contend, offered some protection from societal stigma. Does one embroil oneself, then, in an argument of "sick, but not sorry" or "sorry, but not sick," as did Ettorre (1980) social lesbians? Why and how does one adapt this concept of sameness without falling prey to the same power structure that would obliterate difference and would render lesbians invisible again? Must one accept the view of the respected historian Peter Gay (cited in Duggan, 1986) that gays were happier when they were hidden? According to Gay, not standing out offered one protection from public scrutiny and, therefore, from condemnation.

Sameness offers one invisibility, it is true. It levels out differences and denies who one really is. It would deny the stigma and the history of oppression against gays. Likewise, it would deny consideration of lesbians as a discrete population. Different, they are, and precisely because of that stigma and minority status. To deny stigma is to close one's eyes to the lack of rights accorded lesbians, foremost among which is the right to be different. Those who say, "It makes no different who you sleep with" trivialize lesbianism, reducing it to mere sexuality. And, if they choose, they can close the bedroom door which they've just erected and deny that lesbians do, in fact, exist.

Sameness denies choice. Lesbianism is not merely the choice to open that same bedroom door. It is not a passive acceptance of a sexual predetermination which manifests itself at an early age without one's knowledge or introspection. Lesbianism is a choice, a stance which by its very nature is political whether the individual lesbian chooses to be politically active or not. The lesbian's real choice is a challenge to patriarchy. It is a definite "no" to the sameness of a predetermined role, a unique role made evident by its assignment to women by men. No matter what its variations, this role has one form open to women: companion to, lover of, wife of, mother of man to perpetuate patriarchal capitalism. One is given the illusion of choice, and sameness is that illusion.

This illusion of choice cannot permeate the lesbian community to create an illusion of uniformity. Cohesiveness and unity do not assume that all lesbians are the same, that all lesbian communities are the same, and that all classes, races, and ethnic groups are the same. To deny difference here is to rob one of one's uniqueness and to demand the same conformity patriarchy demands of all women, conformity to a definition foisted on them by men for men. To acknowledge difference does not create aberration, deviance, or divisiveness. To acknowledge difference is to proclaim hope in change and belief in unity.

Why insist on this issue of difference? One gains visibility, that is, the right to be seen. One no longer says, "I am the same as you," but rather, "I am," And in saying "I am," one reclaims one's identity and one's right, not a request, to equal treatment. A large minority, made up of many minorities who stand out in numbers, can demand the rights that are its due: the right to be, to be different, to be in question of oppression, to be right in the name of all minorities and oppressed people.

Whether by an assumption of sameness or of difference, the professional is forewarned against denying the individual lesbian her uniqueness. She is unique, as a woman, as a lesbian, and as a particular individual lesbian, perhaps one of color, perhaps one in an institution, or one under the age of eighteen. The lesbian, on the one hand, is not the same as the non-lesbian woman "except for her choice of sex partner." Moreover, she is not, by the same token, the same as every other lesbian. Her "problem" cannot be assumed to be her lesbianism, unless it is the problem of the professional. Rather than to perpetuate stigma, the professional is urged to pass on the case to another worker.

Who, then, is this individual lesbian? She is a woman who identifies herself with and as a woman, for friendship, spirituality, and erotic (emotional and sexual) love. She is a member of a stigmatized minority with no officially accepted history, no guaranteed civil rights, no societal validation, no prescribed adolescent dating system, no role models, no societally mirrored identity -- in brief, with no officially sanctioned existence. As such, one could anticipate her having conflicts of values, intensified stress, predisposition to alcohol or drugs, difficulty in interpersonal relations, and problems of spontaneity.

One finds, however, a woman of strengths. Independent by the very nature of her choice to identity with women, she has had to stand up for her rights, as an activist, a leader, or a survivor. Coping with stigma, she has developed the skills to deal with prejudice and oppression and has learned to recognize social control in the multi-oppressive (ageist, racist, sexist, classist, heterosexist) policies surrounding her from the voting place to the department store. In 1986, she is learning to be more flexible and more tolerant of difference of all people within and outside the lesbian community. She is, likewise, learning to form coalitions of different factions to celebrate difference and to gain political strength from unity in difference.

Deprived of many traditional resources, maybe even her family, the lesbian has developed a network of alternative resources. As a support system, friends may act as kin or extended family. The lesbian may socialize among them or may go to a lesbian club or restaurant. In addition, lesbian concerts, theater, and poetry readings provide a cultural environment. Health collectives and lesbian (and gay) community centers offer services ranging from support groups to gynecological exams. Various political and sociocultural groups exist (in large cities), often providing activities every night of the week. Moreover, publications and book shops reach basically every interest group within the lesbian community.

Once again, not every lesbian has access to the same resources, nor perhaps, has she had the same type of personal experiences which facilitate her integration as an autonomous lesbian woman. The social worker, therapist, or educator may be called on for various services.

The lesbian may ask for help with stress management, assertiveness training, or communication skills. Her very real and understandable distrust of the medical world may cause her to demand the advocacy of a social worker during medical visits. Likewise, helping the lover obtain visitation rights in a hospital might be a very real need. Legalities involving discriminatory loss of a job or housing are likely to occur, as well as the need for expert witnesses in custody cases. Some lesbians may require help with the coming-out process. Others, who have overwhelmingly internalized stigma, and who are, therefore, conflicted with self-hatred, may seek help for alcohol and drug addition. Lesbian couples may also choose to seek counseling to help self-validate as a couple, to grow as a couple, or to break up. Support groups for a variety of issues ranging from bereavement to disabilities are another distinct possibility for serving the lesbian client.

Whatever the expressed need, the professional who offers services to the lesbian must be supportive of her lesbianism and fully aware of the burden of stigma imposed by society. To deny this difference is to deny the existence and identity of the lesbian. Although the presenting problem may overtly have nothing to do with lesbianism, the worker must be cognizant of potentially internalized stigma impinging on other facets of the lesbian's life. As a result of oppression, a certain degree of "healthy paranoia" (knowing when or with whom to be "out"), can be anticipated. In a similar vein, the lesbian may be distrustful of the worker or the therapist. She may be wondering if this "professional" is different from those who have historically and repeatedly oppressed her and labeled her as deviant.

In the future, what can be done to better service the lesbian client? It has been shown that the lesbian has reason to distrust the helping professions and thus, to underutilize services in mainstream agencies. Moreover, as a "secret" population (Simmel, cited in Ponse, 1978), lesbians are not readily accessible for research which would help define problems and needs. Research reflective of the various minorities within the lesbian world would help to rectify an incomplete picture of the lesbian. However, it is just these "minorities" -- the aged, the young, the lesbian of color, the physically challenged -- who remain more invisible, unreported, and undifferentiated from their non-lesbian age-cohort, ethnic or racial, or illness group. In order to better identify the population, outreach to these groups must be made through leaders within these communities. Sociological studies pursued by members of the community would be of invaluable service as a resource to the helping professions and in the double fight for rights: as lesbians and as old women, as lesbians and as women of color, and so forth. Likewise, general outreach by the helping professions to draw lesbians to the services offered can be better achieved through organizations, institutions, and publications within the lesbian community. Moreover professionals who are lesbians will effect maximum outreach by coming out as lesbians and by working in and through the lesbian community, as well as in mainstream agencies and services.

The worker, whether gay or straight, can best advance the case for lesbian growth by working on educating the general public and professionals and by working for lesbian (gay) rights. In addition to supporting political action by one's vote for supportive policies and candidates, one can reject homophobic speech, jokes about gays and stereotypes which perpetuate false myths and oppression. One can further educate the public by speaking to the lesbian issue in workshops on sexuality, alternative lifestyles, and the "new family," and by including the lesbian perspective on topics ranging from parenting to death and dying.

Attempting policy change or program development for service delivery to lesbian clients may be quite difficult at this time, given the current conservative trend and the general lack of funding available.   Yet, when one incorporates a "lesbian" issue, such as lesbian youth, into a currently favored "charity" or program, such as runaway youth or drug prevention, one stands a better chance of promoting one's ideas.

Specific topics to be developed through research concern the following: a) lesbian couples -- who are they, what is the duration, the values and the structure of their relationships, and how do they compare to heterosexual and gay male couples? b) reconstituted lesbian families and lesbian families with children by AID -- what are the needs, problems, and stigma involved? c) rural and differently-abled lesbians, who and where are they, and what are the special considerations for service to these populations? Programs or projects to be developed would include the establishment of a lesbian (gay) retirement residence, other alternatives in collective living for older lesbians, and housing or shelter for lesbian (gay) youth. A dire need exists for a shelter specifically designed to house lesbian and gay youth, who, for example, are currently not knowingly accepted in any New York City shelter. As the inheritors of and next generation to women who have had an alternative vision of society, many young lesbian women are now being "thrown away." Society continues its trend of labeling as "deviant" or denying the existence of lesbian youth. Needed, then, are the role models, the lesbian foster and adoptive parents who will be visible and claim the identity as lesbian parents of lesbian children in order to combat stigma for them and their children.

Difference has been the raison d'être of this work. It has directed the need for this researcher to study what is being said about and done for lesbians. As gays and as straights, social workers, therapists and educators cannot let difference dictate discrimination. Rather, they must, as Bernice Goodman urges, celebrate difference and celebrate life. The societal oppression which allows the obliteration of lesbians and gays likewise condones the obliteration of blacks, of Jews, or the aged, of the mentally ill child, of anyone who does not conform. As Audre Lorde says, "There can be no hierarchy of oppression," and no one can afford to ignore another oppressed people because he/she is also oppressed. Combatting the stigma due to homophobia can only aid in the fight against multiple oppressions: racism, sexism, ageism, able-ism, and classism. Within any community of likeness, then, there must be room for the identification of and the nurturance of difference. Thus, it is only in the recognition of that difference that growth will occur and that change will be effected.

I.
THE INDIVIDUAL LESBIAN

LESBIAN IDENTITY

History

Altman, D., Vance, C., Vicinus, M., & Weeks, J. (Eds.). (1988). *Homosexuality, which homosexuality?* Amsterdam: Uitgeverij An Dekker/Schorer.

This is a compilation of the most pertinent papers and/or workshops presented at the largest gay and lesbian conference ever held, the 1987 "Homosexuality which homosexuality?" conference at Amsterdam Frei University. Essentialism vs. Social constructionism, the new lens through which scholars view homosexuality is adeptly discussed in Vance's keynote address. Outstanding scholars, practitioners, and activists explore topics ranging from homosexual identity or role to AIDS, therapy, gay theology, historical roots of lesbianism, etc. in the light of this argument.

Bullough V. (1979). *Homosexuality: A history.* New York: New American Library.

A history of homosexuality from the times of ancient Greece to modern day, this work examines etiology, covers the evolution from religious, to legal, to medical, models of deviance. Current day explanations of sexual preference are examined within a context of gay rights. Although there is a chapter on lesbianism, this work deals almost exclusively with men.

Cavin, S. (1985). *Lesbian origins.* San Francisco: Ism.

This work is a creative, scholarly approach to lesbian-feminist theory. Based on a mixture of empirical data and various theories of sexuality, it examines Amazon culture, goddess worship, incest and taboos, sexuality, etc. It provides a good cultural background for work on lesbianism.

Downing, C. (1989). *Myths and mysteries of same-sex love.* New York: Continuum.

In an effort to illuminate lesbian and gay love, Downing explores the myths handed down to us from Freud and Jung and the Greeks. Downing then goes in search of the ancient gods whom, according to Jung, are our diseases. Ending with Plato's encomium to Eros and viewing Eros as paired with death, Downing then closes with a prologue in which she sees AIDS as offering gays and lesbians a unique possibility of working together and celebrating Eros as we learn to help ourselves and others accept death.

Duberman, M., Vicinus, M., & Chauncey, G. (Eds.). (1989). *Hidden from history: Reclaiming the gay and lesbian past.* New York: Meridian.

This anthology groups together outstanding scholars writing on the gay and lesbian past. While there are fewer articles on lesbians than on gay men, this is, in itself, an indication of how hidden and trivialized the experiences of women and lesbians were. Articles discussing lesbians and lesbian themes in Medieval times, in the 19th and 20th centuries and across diverse cultures are discussed against the backdrop of social constructionism.

Duggan, L. (1979).   "Lesbianism and American history: A brief source review." *Frontiers, 4* (3), 80-85.

This article is a brief outline of the development of societal attitudes towards lesbianism. It examines the ways in which histories label lesbians and lesbianism, when and if they mention it at all. Duggan refers to the best works published up to 1979 which provide the historical background and presence previously (and still) denied to lesbianism as a form of social control. The work includes a good bibliography on histories of sexuality and lesbian archives.

Duggan, L. (1986, September 9).   "History between sheets: Politics go under cover." *The Village Voice Literary Supplement*, pp. 13-14.

This article gives a brief summary of recent rulings concerning PWA's (persons with AIDS) and sodomy laws within the historical context of the treatment of gays. Duggan demonstrates the politicization of sexuality in Chief Justice Burger's invoking of centuries of criminal penalties, including death, for sodomy as a precedent for his decision in *Bowers vs. Hardwick* (1986). She goes on to uncover the thin veil from the homophobia in Peter Gay's *The bourgeois experience: Victoria to Freud -- The education of the senses and the tender passion* (1986), a survey of sexual history.

Dynes, W. (Ed.). (1990). *Encyclopedia of homosexuality*. New York: Garland.

This two-volume work is a comprehensive compilation of over 770 entries on homosexuality. Entries range from a few paragraphs on Afghanistan and references to the "beautiful boys" of poetry in that country to lengthy essays on lesbianism. The reader's guide and the index are particularly helpful.

*Faderman, L. (1981).   *Surpassing the love of men: Romantic friendship and love between women from the Renaissance to the present.* New York: William Morrow.

This work is a cultural history of lesbianism or love between women from the sixteenth to the twentieth century. It examines the great tolerance by men of "romantic friendship" between women up until the nineteenth century. This, the author believes, is due to the fact that, until that time, lesbianism was not seen as something sexual, nor as a threat to male supremacy.   As women's emerging independence reached new heights during World War I society began to adopt the views of Freud, Havelock Ellis, and Krafft-Ebing and declared lesbianism a medical deviance. Faderman concludes that, in the 1980s, fewer women allow themselves to be scared off by that form of social control without at least attempting to understand what lesbianism actually is.

Faderman, L. (1991). *Odd girls and midnight lovers.* New York: Columbia University.

This well-documented book is a history of 20th-century lesbian life. Through personal interviews, journal articles, songs, and unpublished manuscripts, Faderman tells the story of the early 20th-century lesbian subculture up to current lesbian politics.

Ferguson, A. (1990). "Is there a lesbian culture?" In J. Allen (Ed.), *Lesbian philosophies and cultures* (pp. 63-89). Albany, NY: State University of New York.

This article demonstrates why an international lesbian culture does not exist. The author calls for the creation of international lesbian movements reflective of pluralism as opposed to one of cultural imperialism.

Katz, J. (1976). *Gay American history: Lesbians and gay men in the U.S.A.* New York: Avon Books.

This work is an interesting collection of articles, letters, and narratives on gays and gay life from colonial times to the 1970s. The author has divided this history into sections on persecution, treatment, struggle for rights, etc., with articles specifically pertaining to women so marked. The footnotes and bibliography are excellent.

Midnight Sun. (1988). "Sex/gender systems in Native North America." In W. Roscoe (Ed.), *Living the spirit* (pp. 32-47). New York: St. Martin's.

This well-written article by an anthropologist, herself an Anishnawbe Indian, serves as an ethnographic approach to gender studies with Native Americans. The author finds social constructionism too limiting a lens with which to view same-gender erotic behavior among native peoples, due to its failure to consider sex/gender within the wider social and economic contexts. She uses case studies of the Mohave, the Navajo, and the Peigan to illustrate native concepts of homosexualities.

*Schwarz, J. (1979). "The lesbian history questionnaire." *Frontiers, 14* (3), 1-12.

Outstanding lesbian theorists and researchers examine issues in the uncovering and the writing of lesbian histories. These histories will fill the "lesbian visibility" gap created to protect heterosexual culture and society. Especially good are the sections on definitions of lesbianism, racism, classism, and homophobia.

Portraits

Adair, N., & Adair, C. (1978). *Word is out: Stories of some of our lives.* New York: Dell.

This work is essentially the script of the film *Word is out.* It includes interviews with the twenty-six lesbians and gay men who come from various racial, ethnic, and class

backgrounds and differing jobs and lifestyles. Missing are
the Native Americans and the physically challenged. The
work includes a good annotated bibliography.

Albro, J., & Tully, C. (1979). "A study of lesbian
lifestyles in the homosexual micro-culture and the
heterosexual macro-culture." *Journal of Homosexuality, 4,*
331-343.

This somewhat dated article examines demographics,
lifestyles, and social relationships of lesbians. The findings
show that most lesbians in the study socialize in the lesbian
community out of a feeling of isolation in the heteroculture.
Yet, they also function productively at work and in
professional organizations in the straight world. Although
desirous of acceptance, most are not willing to "conform" to
pass.

Belote, D., & Joesting, J. (1976). "Demographic and
self-report characteristics of lesbians." *Psychological
Reports, 39,* 621-622.

This brief article reports results of a questionnaire
distributed in gay bars, gathering places, and colleges. It
finds that there is a direct correlation between recognition of
one's lesbianism and self-acceptance. Findings show that
more than 75 percent do not engage in role playing, that 99
percent stated being psychologically healthy, and 63 percent
fear being fired if their employer were to know of their
lesbianism.

*Browning, C. (1984). "Changing theories of
lesbianism: Challenging the stereotypes." In T. Darty & S.
Potter (Eds.), *Women-identified women* (pp. 11-30).
Palo Alto, CA: Mayfield.

This excellent article examines the etiology of
lesbianism from the perspective of traditional biologists and
psychoanalysts. It demonstrates the shortcomings and
fallacies of methodologies used to conclude that the lesbian

possesses male hormones or genes, a psychotic deviance, or an arrest in development. The author offers a social interactionist and feminist perspective, viewing lesbianism as a sequential development of sexuality, a process of assigning and moderating meaning as it is reflected through the interaction of self and others (coming-out); and as an identification with women, a choice that rejects patriarchy's assumption of heterosexuality and traditional sex roles.

Dancy, C. (1990). "The influence of familial and personality variables on sexual orientation in women." *The Psychological Record, 40,* 437-449.

This study examines the effect of personality factors and family attitudes and behaviors on the sexual orientation of lesbian and non-lesbian women. The study concludes that none of the variables acts as a significant predictor of sexual orientation.

Demming, B. (1981). "The lesbian as heretic: An exchange with Leah Fritz." In *Remembering who we are* (pp. 135-147). Tallahassee, FL: Naiad Press.

This article examines the myth that lesbians are not real women. In an attack on patriarchal values, the author defines lesbians as women who choose to love at close quarters with those who recognize themselves as mortals rather than with supposed gods; women who feel that women, as well as men, should be mothered and must be careful to mother their own selves.

Ettorre, E. (1980). *Lesbians, women and society.* Boston: Routledge/Kegan Paul.

The author discusses "social lesbianism," dividing it into "Sapphists" and "Conference" lesbians or born lesbians and political lesbians. At issue is the discussion of how one copes with the label of deviance: by an assertion of one's right to live as a lesbian, or by living one's lesbianism as an activist critic of a "sick" society. While the work seeks to affirm a positive identity for British lesbians and to address the issue of a feminist critique of society, its focus is on the distinction between the two groups of lesbians.

Hersch, P. (1991). "What is gay? What is straight?" *Family Therapy Networker, 15* (1), 40-41.

This brief article examines the dichotomous thinking behind the argument of homosexuality vs. heterosexuality. The author details several clinical cases where individuals have changed behaviors and/or self-labels. She urges homosexuals and heterosexuals not to view sexual orientation as a prison, to focus less on sexual acts and fantasies as the key to personality, and more on relationships that enrich clients' lives.

Lehman, J. (1978). "What it means to love another woman." In G. Vida (Ed.), *Our right to love* (pp. 22-26). Englewood Cliffs, NJ: Prentice-Hall.

An excellent general article on lesbian identity, it exposes certain myths, examines role playing, and differentiates between some gay male and lesbian social habits.

Lewis, S. (1979). *Sunday's women: A report on lesbian life today.* Boston: Beacon Press.

In a general introduction to lesbian life (1979), the author contrasts the current lifestyles and roles to earlier (pre-1955) ways. The major weakness in the work seems to be the author's emphasis on the possible/probable necessity of remaining closeted.

Lockard, D. (1985). "The lesbian community: An anthropological approach." *Journal of Homosexuality, 2* (3), 83-95.

This article defines the lesbian community as a social network of lesbians with a shared group identity, subcultural values and norms interacting in institutionally-based, set places. The author differentiates between the community, the lesbian population, and the lesbian subculture.

Loewenstein, S. (1980). "Understanding lesbian women." *Social Casework, 61* (1), 29-38.

This article is a portrait of the diversification of the lesbian in history, interests, and characteristics. It gives positive images of lesbians, their love relationships, and their friendships. The author suggests that social workers can help lesbians with issues of self-esteem, mediation with parents, and advocacy in court cases.

Resources for Feminist Research, 12 (1).

-- **Geller, G.** (1983). "The issue of nonmonogamy among lesbians." (pp. 44-45).

This article examines monogamy as a lifestyle, as well as the reasons why it is considered "politically incorrect" by some lesbian-feminists. The author examines other alternatives, including the case of two triads.

-- **Quinlan, J.** (1983). "Lesbian relationships." (pp. 50-51).

This brief article examines the meaning of "being a lesbian." It discusses the variety of lifestyles, relationships, and political philosophies existing in the lesbian community.

Risman, B., & Schwartz, P. (1988). "Sociological research on male and female homosexuality." *Annual Review of Sociology, 14,* 125-147.

This article explores four major areas of research on homosexuality: etiology, gender role non-conformity, couple dynamics, and AIDS. The authors summarize a fund of information and demonstrate the need for further research, especially that which focuses on a "sociology of desire" as opposed to a "sociology of homosexuality." The authors fail to include lesbians in the section on AIDS.

Stevens, P., & Hall, J. (1991). "A critical historical analysis of the medical construction of lesbianism." *International Journal of Health Services, 21* (2), 291-307.

This article explores the development of the medicalization of lesbianism from the early sexologists such as Krafft-Ebing to the removal of "Ego dystonic homosexuality" from the *Diagnostic and Statistical Manual of Mental Disorders* in 1987. The authors also discuss the efforts on the part of the gay community to destigmatize homosexuality and to fight for gay rights.

Stone, S. (Ed.). (1990). *Lesbians in Canada*. Toronto, Canada: Between the Lines.

This is a collection of essays of interest to lesbians. Topics range from lesbians in academia to lesbians and the law and disabilities.

Storms, M. (1983). *Development of sexual orientation*. Module of the Community on Gay Concerns. Washington DC: American Psychological Association.

This module examines and discounts the myths concerning the etiology of homosexuality. The author claims that the only consistent findings relevant to the development of homosexuality involve same-sex fantasies, fantasies which existed even during adolescence. Furthermore, he stresses that little is known about the causes of heterosexuality, homosexuality, or preference towards any person.

Terry, J. (1990). "Lesbians under the medical gaze: Scientists search for remarkable differences." *The Journal of Sex Research, 27* (3), 317-39.

This article examines prior research conducted with lesbians in the 1930s to determine which characteristics differentiated them from heterosexual women. The author finds several contradictions in the original research based primarily on the researcher's understanding of lesbians as "masculine" women. The original research saw no way to interpret "feminine" women and female sexuality as separate from men and masculinity.

SELF-LABELING

Coming Out

Chapman, B., & Brannock, J. (1987). "Proposed model of lesbian identity development: An empirical examination." *Journal of Homosexuality, 4* (3-4), 69-80.

This article records the results of a descriptive study of lesbians and lesbian identity. The authors suggest a five-stage model of identity formation, concluding that same-sex attraction precedes awareness of difference and self-labeling as a lesbian.

Darty, T., & Potter, S. (Eds.). (1984). *Women-identified women*. Palo Alto, CA: Mayfield Press.

--***Baetz, R.** (1984). "The coming-out process: Violence against lesbians." pp. 45-51.

This article examines the coming-out process as violence against lesbians since the lesbian struggles against the social controls to keep her in line. In so doing, she risks loss of confidence, of self-esteem, and of economic, legal, and social privilege in the process. The author's nine crossroads of coming out are of utmost use to the counselor in helping the lesbian through the process. Moreover, the counselor will more easily understand the coping skills developed by the lesbian as a result of the coming-out process.

--***Gramick, J.** (1984). "Developing a lesbian identity." pp. 31-45.

This article examines the various theories of lesbian identity and self-labeling. The author posits that signification (self-awareness) and coming out (a developing process) lead to self-acceptance. It includes significant statistics of those sampled for the sequentially staged model. In addition, salient features of lesbian identity (feeling different, experiencing emotional/sexual attraction to another women) are ranked in chronological order demonstrating the need for emotional attraction before physical contact.

Elliott, P. (1985). "Theory and research on lesbian identity formation." *International Journal of Women's Studies, 8*, 64-71.

This article examines lesbian identity formation as a process of awareness and acceptance based on interactionist changes. Through empirical investigation, the author compares the coming-out process in men and in women and finds similarities in events leading to identity formation but differences in the relative importance of these events.

Franke, R., & Leary, M. (1991). "Disclosure of sexual orientation by lesbians and gay men: A comparison of private and public process." *Journal of Social & Clinical Psychology, 10* (3), 262-269.

This article reports on a study conducted with gay men and lesbians exploring predictors of "coming out." Anticipation of rejection or acceptance by others rather than a personal sense of self-acceptance was found to determine willingness to come out by lesbians and gays.

Kahn, M. (1991). "Factors affecting the coming-out process for lesbians." *Journal of Homosexuality, 21* (3), 47-70.

This article reports the results of a study conducted with 81 lesbians using Cass' Stage Allocation Measure and the Openness Questionnaire of Graham et al. Many factors, including differentiation from family of origin, sex-role attitudes, and internalized homophobia were considered. Although congruence in subjective labeling and behavior were established, rate of progression through the stages did not imply integration of behavior.

Resources for Feminist Research, 12 (1).

-- **Elliott, P.** (1983). "Lesbian identity and self-disclosure." pp. 51-52.

This article examines the results of a survey on coming out in which most respondents feel good about having come out. Attention is given to the length of time necessary between coming out and feeling good, the sense of identity, difficulties experienced due to being "out," and degree of politicization.

--**Valverde, M.** (1983). "Beyond guilt: lesbian-feminism and coming out." pp. 65-67.

This excellent article examines coming out from a political perspective. The author discusses the tendency to be absolute, moralistic, and "politically correct" concerning coming out at the risk of alienating others whose psychosocial political conditions do not facilitate their coming out.

Sophie, J. (1986). "A critical examination of stage theories of lesbian identity development." *Journal of Homosexuality, 12* (2), 39-51.

This article examines a general stage theory of lesbian identity, developed from six different theories, as a framework against which to view fourteen lesbian respondents to a questionnaire on coming out. Identity development in these lesbians was not always consistent with the stage theory (awareness, testing, identity acceptance, and integration). Sophie faults the linear nature of the stage theory, as well as her methodology. Although there is no mention of political consciousness, the author does mention cultural contact (Spaulding's theory) and resocialization (Raphael's theory).

Troiden, R. (1988).   "Homosexual identity development." *Journal of Adolescent Health Care, 9* (2), 105-113.

This article presents another stage theory of identity development. Its strength lies in the exploration of defense behaviors or attitudes to manage the stigma/anxiety at each stage of development.

Concept of Self

Allen, J. (Ed.). (1990). *Lesbian philosophies and cultures.* Albany, NY: State University of New York Press.

This collection of essays explores the various aspects of a lesbian philosophy and culture. What is at once apparent is that there is not merely one lesbian community, one politic, one culture. Lesbians of color, working-class lesbians, aging lesbians, lesbians with disabilities, etc. add their voices to this collection, the last section of which contains fiction and journal-type entries.

*Brooks, V. (1981). *Minority stress and lesbian women.* Lexington, MA: Lexington Books.

This is a most intelligent exposé of minority stress as it impacts lesbian women. The result is often lowered self-esteem and, consequently, fewer coping skills to avoid maladaptive behaviors, substance abuse, depression, and suicide. Issues of identity conflict, cognitive dissonance, and cognitive restructuring are examined most astutely and form the thrust of the author's argument: self-redefinition to self-acceptance to acceptance of the reference group. This minority group consciousness further embraces a universal action for all minorities with an incremental growth in self-esteem. This cycle of self-reinforcement can lead to the restructuring of societal attitudes and values to bring our society's system of discriminatory action into consonance with its expressed democratic values system.

DeFries, Z. (1979). "A comparison of political and apolitical lesbians." *Journal of the American Academy of Psychoanalysis, 7* (1), 57-66.

A good example of a study to beware of, this article compares two groups of lesbians -- one political, the other apolitical -- from 1972 to 1977 in an effort to clarify the choice of a lesbian's sexual preference when one does or does not adhere to the prevailing cultural ideology. With an acknowledged lack of methodological rigor, the author finds that her political lesbians were overwhelmingly conflicted over their sexual identity, a choice derived from the outside authority of feminism. She concludes that her respondents are responsible for the stigmatized difference they feel because they have "uncritically" adopted an ideology causing them to reject the examination of the prevailing culture and the security and acceptance it offers.

de Lauretis, T. (Ed.). (1991). "Queer theory." *Differences: A Journal of Feminist Cultural Studies, 3* (2). Providence, RI: Brown University Press.

This scholarly collection of articles on gay and lesbian issues whose focus is primarily literary and philosophical serves as a deconstructionist political analysis.

*Faderman, L. (1984). "The New 'Gay' lesbians." *Journal of Homosexuality, 10* (3), 85-95.

This article differentiates between the old (pre-movement) and the new (movement) lesbians in terms of lesbianism as a radical-feminist political choice. In so examining lesbianism, the author states that lesbian identity formation is achieved through a universalistic stage, that is, a critical evaluation of patriarchal society, a sociocentric stage of feeling isolated outside the lesbian-feminist community, and an egocentric stage of lesbian sexual experience. She likewise discounts the importance of a predetermined orientation manifested through early prepubescent experiences.

Ferguson, D., & Finkler, D. (1978).   "An involvement and overtness measure for lesbians: Its development and relation to anxiety and social zeitgeist." *Archives of Sexual Behavior, 7* (3), 211-228.

This article examines the well-being of lesbians as indicated by the measure in use. The findings show lesbians to be as well and, in some cases, better adjusted than heterosexuals. The authors hypothesize that contending with the label of deviance, if well resolved, may lead to a stronger sense of identity and self-acceptance.

Kitzinger, C. (1988). *The social construction of lesbianism.* Newbury Park, CA: Sage.

This work explores the conflict between the two ideologies which frame the language and goals of feminism and gay rights: liberal humanism and radical lesbian feminism. The author attempts to demonstrate that while liberal humanism would seem to counterattack the "pathological" construct of homosexuality by proposing gay affirmative lifestyle, it privatizes the issue.   The privatization/personalization ultimately adds to the oppression of lesbians since it fails to address the "political" issue of power which is , she says, the real goal of feminists and lesbians.

*Krieger, S. (1985).   "Lesbian identity and community: Recent social science literature." In E. Fredman, B. Gelpi, S. Johnson, & K. Weston (Eds.), *The lesbian issue* (pp. 91-108). Chicago: University of Chicago Press.

This article is a review of the best and the most current social science literature on lesbian identity, that is, as an individual and as a member of a community vis-à-vis society as a whole. Krieger discusses the sense of solidarity and molding of self-esteem within a minority community, as well as the often resultant lack of differentiation within the same community.

*McCoy, S., & Hicks, M. (1979). "A psychological retrospective on power in the contemporary lesbian-feminist community." *Frontiers, 4* (3), 65-69.
This intelligent article examines power within the lesbian community. The authors study the lesbian's need to be included in and her fear of being excluded from the community. They also discuss the formation of lesbian identity within the community, as well as the lesbian's need to develop her personal identity out of confrontation with her human condition and its underlying solitude. This work is important for understanding the stress and possible alienation of new lesbians trying to contact the lesbian community.

Moses, A. (1978). *Identity management in lesbian women.* New York: Praeger.
This work treats the issues of visibility as a lesbian and lesbian risk-taking in the management of one's lesbian identity. Based on studies, the author claims that lesbians experience more difficulty in coping the more they believe they will be discovered as lesbians.

Nichols, M., & Leiblum, S. (1986). "Lesbianism as a personal identity and social role: A model." *Affilia, 1* (1), 45-58.
The authors examine the argument for "identity and social role" as opposed to the medical or sexual preference model. This model focuses on the lesbian's self-labeling, living, and loving behavior within her "outsider status" (rejection of the traditional role for women and rejection by homophobic society) as the major components of a lesbian identity.

Phelan, S. (1989). *Identity politics: Lesbian feminism and the limits of community*. Philadelphia: Temple University Press.

This work represents an evolving analysis of lesbian feminism as a political philosophy capable of encompassing the concepts of the individual and the community. The author's argument interprets radical feminism as a "totalist" reaction to liberalism and, therefore, incapable of supporting difference. The issue of (lesbian) sexuality has been dropped from discourse, says the author, and lesbian S/M advocates and other sexual minorities are now oppressed by those who reacted against their oppression as women. A difficult, often abstruse political analysis, this book concludes with a deconstructionist analysis of the self and the determination that rather than to totally dismiss liberalism, one must adapt it to accommodate "communitarianism" and individualism.

Ponse, B. (1976). "Secrecy in the lesbian world." *Urban Life*, *5* (3), 313-337.

This article treats the lesbian community as a "secret society" as described by the sociologist Simmel. Secrecy would, then, typify the lesbian's interactions with other lesbians, with the lesbian community, and between the lesbian community and society. Issues of coming out, passing for heterosexual, denial (counterfeit secrecy), disclosure, verbal and nonverbal cues on self-identifying, etc. are discussed. The author's later work is more refined on this topic and omits the stereotyping into "butch" and "femme."

*Ponse, B. (1978). *Identities in the lesbian world*. Greenport, CT: Greenwood Press.

Examining how lesbian identity is constructed, the author rejects both the consistency-essentiality sickness model of heterosexual society and the gay trajectory-essentiality model of the lesbian community. According to Ponse, both theories do not allow for change over time and associate identity too closely with behavior. She stresses the meaning which the individual attributes to her identity and categorizes four possible combinations of hetero-homosexual behavior and signification.

Weitz, R. (1984). "From accommodation to rebellion: The politicization of lesbianism." In T. Darty & S. Potter (Eds.), *Women-identified women* (pp. 233-249). Palo Alto, CA: Mayfield.

This work traces the development of lesbian group identity through a rejection of labeling and stigma over the years. It examines historical events and the creation and evolution of gay and lesbian social groups. The author discusses lesbianism as a choice in response to a sexist society.

II.
MINORITIES WITHIN A MINORITY

LESBIANS OF COLOR / THIRD WORLD LESBIANS

Allen, P.G. (1986). *The sacred hoop: Recovering the feminine in American Indian traditions.* Boston: Beacon Press.

This book is a collection of essays about women's place in Native American culture. Allen discusses Indian women's history, female deities, and the respected position of lesbians within the circle of Indian life.

*Catalyst, 12, (1981).

   -- Garcia-Vida, M. "The Cuban exodus -- reality and propaganda." pp. 91-102.

This article examines the experiences of Cuban refugees in fleeing Cuba. The author also discusses the nature of the extreme oppression of gays and lesbians in Cuba. The article is helpful in understanding the total framework/environment of the Cuban refugee lesbian.

   -- Monteflores, C. "Conflicting allegiances: Therapy issues with Hispanic lesbians." pp. 31-36.

This article examines several guidelines which are pertinent to recognizing and respecting the self-definition of the Hispanic lesbian as an individual within the group. These issues involve primary identification (as a lesbian or as an ethnic) socioeconomic and educational needs, degree of feminist consciousness, and degree of overtness.

Chan, C. (1989). "Issue of identity development among Asian-Americans." *Journal of Counseling & Development, 68* (1), 16-20.

This article records the results of a survey on identity with 35 gay and lesbian Asian-Americans. The author discusses discrimination as gays and as Asians and difficulty of coming-out, especially to parents because of the implied rejection of Asian culture.

Cornwell, A. (1983). *Black lesbian in white America.* Tallahassee, FL: Naiad Press.

This work includes some of Cornwell's outstanding essays on the black lesbian. They examine the difficulties of the black lesbian in a male-dominated, homophobic, conservative black community and a white racist world. Cornwell also decries the racism within the women's movement.

Darty, T., & Potter, S. (Eds.). (1984). *Women-identified women.* Palo Alto, CA: Mayfield Press.

-- Allen, P.G. (1984). "Beloved women: The lesbian in American Indian culture." pp. 83-97.

This work examines matriarchy and women's medicine in traditional American Indian culture. The author makes the argument for the existence and acceptance of lesbian women among American Indians. She claims that the Judeo-Christian tradition and fear of women's power have led to the suppression of virtually all information on "koskalaka" (women who do not wish to marry).

-- Brant, B. (1984). "Reclamation: A lesbian Indian story." pp. 97-105.

A personal account of the coming-out process of a mixed Indian-white mother, this work deals with the racism and classism within the women's movement and the author's own internalized racism.

-- **Hidalgo, H.** (1984). "The Puerto Rican lesbian in the United States." pp. 105-117.
This article represents the findings of a study conducted with 300 Puerto Rican lesbians. It provides a general profile of the Puerto Rican lesbian in the United States. Also included is Bernice Goodman's guide for selecting a non-homophobic therapist.

Fitzgerald, L. (1977). "Lesbianism among Blacks." *Brown Sister, 4,* 15-21.
This article examines the black lesbian experience and compares it to that of a white lesbian. The author discusses the parallel experiences, both lesbian but each peculiar to its race.

Gay American Indians, & Roscoe, W. (1988). *Living the spirit.* New York: St. Martin's.
This anthology contains well-written and well-balanced selections of fiction, nonfiction, oral tradition, poetry, and personal narratives which address homosexuality, lesbianism, berdache cross-gender roles, and cross-dressing among Native Americans. Treating the past and traditional ways, the first section contains much anthropological material. The second part examines gay Native Americans today. The writers, representative of many different Native American peoples, view cross-gender roles and cross-dressing in relation to the social organization of the period of the people studied.

Gibbs, J., & Bennett, S. (Eds.). (1980). *Top ranking: A collection of articles on racism and classism in the lesbian community.* Brooklyn, NY: February 3rd Press.

This is a collection of articles written by black and white lesbians on racism, classism, and homophobia. They explore the oppression in heterosexual society as well as within the lesbian community, and especially, in prisons.

Hidalgo, H., &Christensen, E. (1976). "The Puerto Rican lesbian and the Puerto Rican Community." *Journal of Homosexuality, 2* (3), 109-121.

This article takes a look at Puerto Rican lesbians from both the perspective of the lesbian and of the heterosexual. The lesbians in this study express great fear of being discovered by the heterosexuals who portray her as sick and "butch." More information on Puerto Rican lesbians, which is sorely needed, is most difficult to obtain because of the lack of visibility on the part of the most closeted, apolitical Puerto Rican lesbian.

Interracial Books for Children Bulletin, 14 (3).
    -- Lorde, A. (1983). "There is no hierarchy of oppression." p. 9.

This is a most persuasive article on the interconnectedness of homophobia, sexism, and racism. Lorde stresses the fact that those who are multi-oppressed cannot profit from the oppression of any part of one's identity, and that, therefore, no oppressed group can allow the oppression of any other minority group.

    -- Smith, B. (1983). "Homophobia: Why bring it up?" pp. 7-8.

This article examines the myths surrounding homosexuality in the black community. Homosexuality is seen by traditional blacks as the wealthy white disease, and homophobia, as a minor, rightful oppression.

    -- Tinney, J. (1983). "Interconnections." pp. 4-6.

The author examines the intertwining of racism, sexism, and homophobia, as well as institutional, collective, and individual oppressions.

Jones, A.B. (1983). "The need for cultural sensitivity in working with third world lesbian and gay youth." In S. Bergstrom & L. Cruz (Eds.), *Counseling lesbian and gay youth* (pp. 69-75). San Francisco: National Network.

This brief article examines the chief conflicts in the consciousness of a third world gay youth: ethnicity/race or gayness. The author describes the attitude of the black and Hispanic community towards homosexuality as being a sin, a political ploy, or genocide at the hands of the white community.

Loiacano, D. (1989). "Gay identity issues among Black Americans: Racism, homophobia, and the need for validation." *Journal of Counseling & Development, 68* (1), 21-25.

This article briefly outlines the major obstacles to black gay/lesbian identity development. Acceptance in the black community and in the gay community, and the integration of both aspects of one's identity are the three themes which emerge from open-ended interviews with six participants in this study.

Lorde, A. (1984). *Sister Outsider*. Trumansburg, NY: Crossing Press.

These essays examine the multi-oppression of the black lesbian as a black, as a woman, as a lesbian. She is oppressed by whites and blacks, heterosexuals and by white lesbians. She calls for unity within difference to fight all oppression. Particularly effective in this area are the essays "Age, race, class, and sex: Women redefining difference" and "Scratching the surface: Some notes on barriers to women and loving."

*Moraga, C., & Anzaldua, G. (1981). *This bridge called my back: Writings by radical women of color.* Watertown, MA: Persephone Press.

A collection of fiction and nonfiction by Native American Indians, blacks, Latinas, and Asian Americans, the works range from essays on homophobia, racism, and classism to poetry on violence and alienation. Noteworthy are the works by Cameron, speaking of the oppression of the gay Native American; Clarke, who likens heterosexism to colonialism; and Barbara and Beverly Smith, on multi-oppressions and the homophobia of the Black community.

Morales, E. (1990). "Ethnic minority families and minority gays and lesbians." In F. Bozett, & M. Sussman (Eds.), *Homosexuality and family relations* (pp. 217-239). New York: Harrington Park Press.

This chapter explores the double stigma of being gay or lesbian and an ethnic minority. Goffman's theory of minority social interaction stress is discussed, as is the attitude of both minorities toward each other. A "Coming-out" state (sexual and ethnic) theory is developed, and implications for therapy are given.

Noda, B., Tusi, K., & Wong, Z. (1979), (Spring). "Coming out: We are here in the Asian community: A dialogue with three Asian women." *Bridge: An Asian-American Perspective*, pp. 22-24.

This article examines the personal accounts of coming out by three Asian American lesbians. The pressures from the traditional extended family and the need for activism as third world people are discussed. The authors call for visibility as lesbians since strength as Asian lesbians strengthens the whole third world movement, homo- and heterosexual.

Omosupe, E. (1991). "Black/lesbian/bulldagger." *Differences, 3* (2), 101-112.

This article succinctly outlines the major themes of Black lesbian identity as a position of silence, erasure, and oppression by the dominant white male culture as well as by the white lesbian community. The author sees black lesbian identity as one of resistance and calls for black lesbians to define themselves to fight their obliteration by whites.

Ramos, J. (Ed.). (1987). *Companeros: Latina lesbians*. New York: Latina Lesbian History Project.

This is an anthology of mostly unpublished Latina lesbians on a variety of topics including Latina lesbian identity.

Rich, B., & Arguelles, L. (1985). "Homosexuality, homophobia, and revolution: Notes toward an understanding of the Cuban lesbian and gay male experience, Part II." *Signs, 10,* 120-135.

This article analyzes the interaction of the political and economic issues of the enclaves, processes of transculturation, and the manipulation of the Cuban gay issue by anti-Castro organizations and the United States government. Based on this understanding, an effective outreach to this gay community in the United States can be made across the barriers of isolation and the racism/classism within the white gay community.

Trujillo, C. (Ed.). (1991). *Chicana lesbians*. Berkeley, CA: Third Woman Press.

This anthology of first person accounts, interviews, fiction, poetry, and analytical essays explores the question of who the Chicana lesbian is. The well-balanced and well-written selections portray the rich and diversified experience of the Chicana lesbian caught among the worlds of heterosexual Latinos, of dominant (white) heterosexuals, and the (white) lesbian community.

Organizations

African Ancestral Lesbians United for Societal Change
(formerly Salsa Soul Sisters)
       Gay and Lesbian Community Services Center
        208 West 13th Street
       New York, NY 10011
       (212) 620-7310

Gay American Indians (GAI)
       1347 Divisadero St. #312
       San Francisco, CA 94115
       (415) 621-3485

National Coalition of Black Lesbians and Gays
       930 F Street, N.W.
       Suite 514
       Washington, DC 20004

Oakland Black and Third World Gays
       5960 Racine Street
       Oakland, CA 94609
       (415) 654-7818

Ombahee River Collective
       149 Windsor Street #3
       Cambridge, MA 02139
       (617) 661-4104

South Asian Lesbian and Gay Association/SALGA
       Gay and Lesbian Community Services Center
       208 West 13th Street
       New York, NY 10011

Third World Gay/Lesbian Counseling Professionals
       c/o Operation Concern
       Pacific Medical Center

1853 Market Street
San Francisco, CA 94103
(415) 626-7000

Third World Lesbian and Gay Conference
      P.O. Box 548
      Columbia, MD 21094
      (202) 797-8877

AGING

Adelman, M. (1980). "Adjustment to aging and styles of being gay: A study of elderly gay men and lesbians" (Doctoral Dissertation, Wright Institute, 1979). *Dissertation Abstracts International, 40,* p. 92.

   This study examines the aging process in gay men and lesbians over 60 years of age. The findings show that there is no significant difference in the process of aging between heterosexuals and homosexuals with the exception of the impact of stigma on homosexuals.

Adelman, M. (Ed.). (1986). *Longtime Passing: Lives of older lesbians.* Boston: Alyson.

   This is a collection of articles and interviews about lesbians 60-85 years of age. They discuss past and present lives, concerns over aging, and changes in gay lifestyle.

Adelman, M. (1990). "Stigma, gay lifestyle, and adjustment to aging: a study of later-life gay men and lesbians." *Journal of Homosexuality, 20* (3-4), 7-32.

   This article records the results of a study conducted with older lesbians and gays. An expansion of earlier research, the study examines age of discovery of one's gayness, self-definition and disclosure, and involvement with other gays as potential indicators of later-life satisfaction and adjustment to aging. Findings show that those who discovered their gayness earlier and disclosed less, were more likely to be satisfied and adjust well to aging. The author feels that secrecy has provided security and support to this pre-Stonewall group of aging gays.

Alexander, J., Berrow, D., Domitrovich, L., Donnelly, M., & McLean, C. (Eds.). (1986). *Women and aging.* Corvallis, OR: Calyx Books.

In this anthology on aging, the works range from poetry to essays to reviews. Notable are the essays by Macdonald and Cooper and the interviews with Macdonald and Rich. They attack the ageism prevalent in social agencies and call for changes in the economic and social systems which oppress aging women.

*Almvig, C. (1982). *The invisible minority: Aging and lesbianism.* Utica, NY: Institute of Gerontology, Utica College of Syracuse.

This study of 74 lesbians over the age of 50 examines their attitudes toward aging, their lesbianism, and interaction in the lesbian and hetero communities. The findings show that most respondents have a positive attitude toward aging, and are sexually active, and are solidly connected to their support network of friends.

Berger, R. (1982). "The unseen minority: Older gays and lesbians." *Social Work, 27* (3), 236-242.

This is a comprehensive article on the special needs and strengths of aging gays. Berger finds that the strength of gays lies in their successfully having overcome stigma and their friendship networks. Also, in same-sex couples, one is less likely to lose a partner to an earlier death because of a difference in life expectancy between the sexes.

Disadvantages of being gay arise from discriminatory practices in medical, legal, and retirement institutions.

*Copper, B. (1985). "The view from over the hill: Notes on ageism between lesbians." *Trivia*, *7*, 48-63. *(Trivia*, P.O. Box 606, North Amherst, MA 01059).

This article examines ageism within the lesbian community as a major barrier to claiming lesbian identity. Ageism, as a structure of patriarchy, prevents powerful women from challenging male power, and matriarchal values and lineage from threatening the male position. From her place of invisibility, the old woman is disempowered vis-à-vis the male population, as well as the lesbian population. The author calls for self-examination to wage a campaign against ageism and to integrate older lesbians into the full process of lesbian life.

*DeCecco, J.,   Kehoe, M.,   & Goldberg, S. (1984).   "Lesbians over 60:   A national survey." Unpublished research report of the Center for Research and Education in Sexuality, San Francisco, CA.

This study, based on questionnaires from 100 lesbians aged 60-85, finds the aging lesbian to be a well-adjusted, happy, productive woman whose greatest problem is occasional loneliness. Most socialize with lesbians of their own age, and others with lesbians not more than ten years younger or older. This socialization takes place within one's circle of friends and not in bars.

Deevey, S. (1990). "Older lesbian women -- An invisible minority." *Journal of Gerontological Nursing, 16* (5), 35-39.

This article records the results of a study on aging conducted with 78 lesbians. The results are helpful to nurses (and other health care workers) working with aging lesbians, especially since many older lesbians will not disclose their lesbianism to health care workers.

Friend, R. (1987).   "The individual and social responsibility of aging: Clinical implications for lesbians and gay men." *Journal of Homosexuality, 14* (1-2), 307-331.

This article summarizes some basic issues of aging for gay men and women. The author helps to combat stereotypical views of the isolated, bitter gay, counters with some of the advantages over heterosexuals enjoyed by gays as they age, and explores "accelerated aging" at length. Unfortunately, much of the material is more pertinent to gay men than to lesbians.

*Friend, R. (1990).   "Older lesbian and gay people: A theory of successful aging." *Journal of Homosexuality, 20* (3-4), 99-118.

This article approaches homosexuality and aging from a social constructionist framework. The author sees lesbians and gays on a continuum from homophobic to passing to positively identified as lesbians and gay men. Those who have reconstructed a negative identity to a positive one have managed crisis competence, potential loss of family, development of new social networks, flexibility in gender roles and general resistance to social norms. Thus, they are better equipped to manage aging.

*Galassi, F. (1991). "A life-review workshop for gay and lesbian elders." *Journal of Gerontological Social Work, 46 (*1-2), 75-86.

This article discusses the development of a life-review model for gay and lesbian elders resulting from a workshop conducted in 1984 at the Gay and Lesbian Services Center in Los Angeles. The intergenerational workshop focused on five areas: homosexual mythology and iconographs, homosexuals and their families (biological and non-biological), coming-out, the homosexual health agenda, and homosexual spiritual perspectives. The findings would serve as a guide to the needs of this population for health care providers.

Gray, D. (1987). "Women's sexuality: From the margin to the center (older lesbians)." *Dissertation Abstracts International, 48,* 1707A.

    This study was conducted with 10 lesbians over the age of 50 to gather information about their past and present lives. Based on in-depth interviews, the author reports that for these lesbians sexuality and sexual orientation is an on-going process, constantly modified by interaction with the dominant culture. The social constructionist view of lesbianism is challenged in this study.

Gwenwald, M. (1984). "The SAGE model for serving older lesbians and gay men." In R. Schoenberg, R. Goldberg, & D.A. Shore (Eds.), *With compassion toward some* (pp. 53-61). New York: Harrington Park Press.

    This article examines SAGE's (the best resource for working with the older lesbian in the NY area) program for the aging gay. In addition to monthly socials, rap groups and other groups, SAGE (Senior Action in a Gay Environment) provides friendly visitor and telephone reassurance service to homebounds.

Kehoe, M. (1985, January). "Uncovering older lesbians." *Bridges*, pp. 38-40.

    This interview examines the difficulty in finding lesbians, especially third world lesbians, for studies whose purpose would be to present data to social agencies to demonstrate the need for special services for the aging lesbian. The author speaks of special retirement housing and legal services as discrete needs.

Kehoe, M. (1986). "Lesbians over 65: A triply invisible minority" and "A portrait of the older lesbian." *Journal of Homosexuality, 12* (3-4), 139-152, and 157-161.

These articles represent the results of Kehoe's survey conducted with 50 lesbians over the age of 65. She draws the portrait of a middle-to-upper middle class, white, well-educated, healthy, active woman who does not frequent gay bars or engage in role playing. Kehoe's findings support her hypothesis that the lesbian over 65 is a "survivor" and thus, better equipped than her heterosexual counterpart to cope with the demands of aging.

Kehoe, M.   (1989). *Lesbians over 60 speak for themselves*. New York: Harrington Park Press.

Based on a 1984 study of 100 lesbians over the age of 60, this book explores the historical background (1900-1950) of participants, their relationships with their families and friends, their sexual relationships, and their aging processes. It also compares Kehoe's study to that of Berger on gay men. The profile of the over-60 lesbian is that of a well-adjusted white middle class professional who currently is not involved sexually, but who had previously had long-term relationships, and whose chief concern is loneliness. The appendix includes a copy of the questionnaire.

*Kimmel, D., Raphael, S., Catalano, D., & Robinson, M. (1984). "State of the art essay: Older lesbians and gay men." Unpublished paper prepared for the 1984 National Gay and Lesbian Health Conference, New York, NY.

This paper presents a positive profile of the aging gay and lesbian. Studies show that they remain active and satisfied with their lifestyles. The authors note that there are certain advantages to being gay because of their successfully coping with stigma. Because of homophobia, there is still a great deal of secrecy which surrounds gays, and as a result, many gays underutilize mainstream programs.

Kirkpatrick, M. (1989). "Middle age and the lesbian experience." *Women's Studies Quarterly, 17* (1-2), 87-96.

This article explores certain women's issues at mid-life from the perspective of the lesbian. The author examines motherhood, childlessness, the need for intimacy, degree of sexuality, fear of intimacy, and illness as they impact lesbians as well as how they are experienced differently by lesbians and non-lesbians.

Laner, M. (1979). "Growing older female: Heterosexual and homosexual." *Journal of Homosexuality, 4* (3), 267-275.

The results of a study carried out by means of personal want ads, this article shows that older lesbians suffer less accelerated aging, do not seek younger mates, and tend to stay in touch with the lesbian community after a break-up.

Lipman, A. (1986). "Homosexual relations." *Generations, 10* (2), 51-54.

A well-intentioned article which sets out to find similarities in homosexual and heterosexual aging couples, it sees as germane the need for love, intimacy, commitment, and companionship. Unfortunately, most of the data is extrapolated from studies on gay men or from heterosexual couples, and stigma is not emphasized as a major difference causing a lack of or underutilization of services.

Lucco, A. (1986). "Planned retirement housing preferences of older gay men and lesbians: Summary report." (available from Lucco, Asst. Medical Director, Levindale Geriatric Center, 2434 W. Belvedere Ave., Baltimore, MD 21215-5299).

This report examines the retirement housing needs of older (55+) gay men and lesbians. Over 88 percent of the respondents expressed interest in a continuing care retirement community (combined shelter/health care facility where participants live independently, but participate collectively in many activities).

Macdonald, B., & Rich, C. (1983). *Look me in the eye.* San Francisco: Spinsters, Ink.

This collection of essays provides a good mixture of theory and personal accounts of ageism and heterosexism. Especially good are "An Open letter to the women's movement" and "Exploitation by Compassion."

Martin, D., & Lyon, P. (1979). "The older lesbian." In B. Berzon & R. Leighton (Eds.). *Positively Gay* (pp. 134-145). Millbrae, CA: Celestial Arts.

This chapter examines the strengths and needs of gays. Among them are legal advocacy, networking with other gays, and advocacy for services by Senior Citizen centers. Loneliness and isolation, especially in rural areas, and death and dying are discussed.

Poor, M. (1982). "Older lesbians." In M. Cruikshank (Ed.), *Lesbian Studies: Present and future* (pp. 165-174). Old Westbury, NY: Feminist Press.

This chapter examines the special characteristics, needs, interests, groups, and outreach to lesbian women over 65. Special concerns are nursing homes, wills, acknowledgment of partner's desires as opposed to those of the family in life/death matters.

Raphael, S., & Robinson, M. (1980). "The older lesbian: Love relationships and friendship patterns." *Alternate Lifestyles, 3* (2), 107-209.

This article represents the results of a study of 20 lesbians over the age of 50. The findings show the older lesbian to be a positive role model who adapts well to aging and who is well supported by a network of friends.

Raphael, S., & Robinson, M. (1981). "Lesbians and gay men in later life." *Generations, 6* (3), 16-18.

This article examines and compares various aspects of gay and lesbian aging: love relationships and sexuality, adjustment to aging, and oppressiveness of nursing homes. Implications for the creation of programs are given.

*Robinson, M. (1979). *The older lesbian.* San Francisco: National Association for Lesbian and Gay Gerontology.

The author studies the adjustment to aging, kinship and friendship networks, and identity of lesbians. The lesbian is seen as a well-adjusted, active woman whose relationship with her family often depends on her degree of overtness. Friendship networks tend to replace kinship where there is no tie to one's family. There is an important discussion on collective living as a potential future lifestyle for aging lesbians.

Sang, B., Smith, A., & Warshow, J. (Eds.). (1991). *Lesbians at midlife: The creative transition.* San Francisco: Spinsters Book Company.

This anthology is a well-written collection of fiction, non-fiction, and poetry on issues pertinent to lesbians over 50. The editors have divided the book thematically: changes, loss, kinship, mother/daughter, partnerships, health and sexuality, spirituality, and the future. Within each section, the articles represent a multiplicity of cultural, ethnic, and racial viewpoints on each topic.

Wolf, D. (1978, November). "Close friendship patterns of older lesbians." Paper presented at the Gerontological Society Meeting, Dallas, TX.

This paper examines how older lesbians manage their lives and how close friendships function as the equivalent of family. The qualities of intimacy, reliability, and confidence are stressed in friendships lasting long periods of time. Friends are the support system during illness, disability, loss, and death of a partner. The author shows uplifting respondents confronting life with spirit and dignity with the help of friends.

Organizations

National Association of Lesbian and Gay Gerontology
      1290 Sutter Street, Suite 8
      San Francisco, CA 94109

Senior Action in a Gay Environment (SAGE)
      208 East 13th Street
      New York, NY 10011
      (212) 741-2247

YOUTH

Alyson, S. (Ed.). (1980). *Young, gay and proud!* Boston: Alyson Publications. (Available from Carrier Pigeon, 75 Kneeland St., Room 1506, Boston, MA 02111).
      This is a collection of letters and personal narratives by gay youth.   Issues dealt with include coming out to friends and parents, stigma, isolation, etc.

Ashkinazy, S. (1984).   "Working with gay and lesbian youth." *Practice Digest, 7* (1), 21-23.
      This article examines the services of the Institute for the Protection of Lesbian and Gay Youth in New York. IPLGY reaches this population through referrals from schools, treatment centers, and courts and self-referrals from ads in newspapers. Services include rap groups, individual

counseling, G.E.D., career, and vocational counseling, and placement in residences, halfway houses, and foster homes.

Bell, R. (1980). *Changing bodies, changing lives: A book for teens on sex and relationships.* New York: Random House.

In this collection of stories, anecdotes, and articles by and about youth, the focus is on physical and emotional health, relationships, and sexuality. Stories on exploring sexuality deal with same-sex and opposite sex relations. The chapter on gay youth discusses coming out and issues in relationships.

*Bergstrom, S., & Cruz, L. (Eds.). (1983). *Counseling lesbian and gay male youth: Their special lives/special needs.* San Francisco: National Network of Runaway Youth Services.

This excellent collection of articles examines various critical issues: coming out, family therapy, rural and third world gay youth. There are good articles on runaway youth, the setting up of programs in shelters and foster homes, and peer support groups.

*Borhek, M. (1988). "Helping gay and lesbian adolescents and their families: A mother's perspective." *Journal of Adolescent Health Care, 9* (2), 123-128.

This article, written by the parent of a gay son, explores the process of self-disclosure by gay adolescents to their parents. It addresses the feelings experienced by the youth as well as by his/her parents.

Boxer, A., & Cohler, B. (1989). "The life course of gay and lesbian youth. An immodest proposal for the study of lives." *Journal of Homosexuality, 17,* (3-4), 315-355.

This article challenges many assumptions about the development of gay and lesbian youth and methods of study, primarily reliance on respondents' recollections regarding their childhood.

Browning, C. (1987). "Therapeutic issues and intervention strategies with young adult lesbian clients: A developmental approach." *Journal of Homosexuality, 14* (1-2), 45-52.
    This article uses an Eriksonian developmental model to explore identity formation by young lesbians. Issues of separation and competence are discussed.

*Cates, J. (1987). "Adolescent sexuality: Gay and lesbian issues." *Child Welfare, 66* (4), 353-363.
    This article discusses therapeutic interventions with adolescents expressing concern about sexual issues. The author stresses that the therapist must address the needs of the adolescent. Pertinent case material is aptly presented to differentiate between a youth whose homosexual behavior represents exploration and another whose behavior indicates a same-sex preference.

*Gonsiorek, J. (1988). "Mental health issues of gay and lesbian adolescents." *Journal of Adolescent Health Care, 9* (2), 114-122.
    This article discusses gay and lesbian sexuality within the context of culturally defined developmental issues. While stressing the negative impact of a homophobic environment on gay youth, the author underlines denial of one's homosexuality and internalized homophobia as factors which may further adversely affect the development of social skills of gay youth. The author calls for support groups, family support, lesbian and gay role models, advocacy, and education.

*Hanckel, F., & Cunningham, J. (Eds.). (1979). *A way of love, a way of life: A young person's introduction to* *what it means to be gay.* New York: Lothrop, Lee and Shepard.

This most comprehensive book offers invaluable information for youth on a range of topics. It addresses name-calling, how to tell if you're gay, coming out, legal issues, etc. The chapter on coming out is excellent.

Hart, J. (1984). *So you think you're attracted to the same sex.* Harmondsworth, England: Penguin.

This book is an informative examination of the gay lifestyle for young lesbians. It deals with sex, sexuality, relationships, identity, and coming out to parents.

*Herdt, G. (1989). *Gay and lesbian youth.* New York: Harrington Park Press.

This collection of articles written by anthropologists, sociologists, and psychologists combines theories of identity formation, cross-cultural coming-out narratives, and studies of gay youth groups in the United States. Emphasis is placed on cultural and environmental factors impacting youth, and the need for longitudinal studies is underlined.

Heron, A. (Ed.). (1983). *One teenager in ten.* Boston: Alyson Publications.

This is a collection of personal narratives of young lesbian women (and gay youth) aged 11-20. These articles express confusion, fear, and doubt. An affirmative response for young lesbians, the book also suggests resources to help parents deal with this issue.

Hersch, P. (1991). "Secret lives." *Family Therapy Networker, 15* (1), 37-43.

This article addresses the experiences of gay adolescents faced with the question of whether or not they are gay , and what to do about it. The author explores the emotions of all involved: the adolescent, his/her friends, and family, and illustrates his points with specific case material.

Hetrick, E., & Martin, A. D.   (1987).
"Developmental issues and their resolution for gay and
lesbian adolescents." *Journal of Homosexuality, 14* (1-2),
25-43.
          This article discusses developmental issues of gay
youth as members of a stigmatized minority. The authors
explore the obstacles to successful identity formation and the
coping mechanisms developed to overcome them.

Hunter, J. (1990). "Violence against lesbian and gay
youth." *Journal of Interpersonal Violence, 5* (3), 295-300.
          This article records the results of a study conducted
with the first 500 applicants for service at the Hetrick-Martin
Institute in New York, a social services agency for gay
youth. Of these, 41 percent reported having suffered
violence by peers, families, or strangers, of which 46
percent was gay related. 41 percent of the girls and 34
percent of the boys subsequently attempted suicide.

Hunter, J. & Martin, A. (1984). "A comparison of the
presenting problems of homosexually and non-
homosexually oriented young people at a student run health
service." Unpublished paper. (Available from IPLGY,
Youth Aid and Education Services, 112 East 23rd St., 4th
floor, New York, NY 10010).
          This paper examines major differences between gay
and straight youth as they presented their problems at Hunter
Student Health Society between 1979 and 1981. Findings
show that gays were younger and had more problems with
family over questions of sexuality. Although untroubled by
their homosexuality per se, they expressed great fear of
homophobic societal pressures, harassment, and violence.
Over 11 percent of the lesbians were most concerned over
emergency housing or problems with shelters.

Hunter, J., & Schaecher, R. (1987). "Stresses on lesbian and gay adolescents." *Social Work in Education, 9* (3), 180-190.

This article outlines the major areas of difficulty for gay youth coming to an awareness of their same-sex preference. The authors discuss the isolation and harassment experienced by gay youth as well as the often resultant suicidal feelings. Implications for school social work practice are drawn.

Jacobsen, E. (1988). "Lesbian and gay adolescents." *Social Worker, 56* (2), 65-67.

This Canadian article addresses the needs of gay and lesbian youth. The author discusses what social workers can do to familiarize themselves with gay youth and to divest themselves of homophobic attitudes.

Krysiak, G. (1987). "A very silent and gay minority." *School Counselor 34* (5), 304-307.

This brief article discusses the role of the school counselor in identifying and counseling gay youth. It encourages counselors to familiarize themselves with ways in which they can help gay students feel more supported and connected with others.

*Martin, A.D. (1982). "Learning to hide: The socialization of the gay adolescent." In S.C. Feinstein, J.G. Looney, A.Z. Schwartzberg, & A.D. Sorosky (Eds.), *Adolescent psychology: Developmental and clinical studies.* Chicago: University of Chicago Press. (pp. 52-65).

This chapter examines the effects of homophobia on gay youth: the necessity for secrecy, the lack of role models, and the lack of a socially validated courting procedure. These may in turn lead to a separation of the emotions from the sexual behavior or an all-too-sudden falling in love and forming of a relationship.

Mercier, L., & Berger, R. (1989). "Social service needs of lesbian and gay adolescents: Telling it their way." *Journal of Social Work & Human Sexuality, 8* (1), 75-95.

This article discusses the results of a study conducted with 49 lesbian and gay adolescents aged 13-21 in Orange County, California to ascertain needs and psychosocial difficulties related to being gay, coming-out issues, and use of social service and gay/lesbian agencies. Although many faced difficulties coping with homophobia, and completing developmental tasks, few availed themselves of services, whether gay/lesbian or traditional mental health. The authors call for greater outreach to this community.

*Needham, R. (1977). "Casework intervention with a homosexual adolescent." *Social Casework 58* (7), 387-394.

This article examines practical issues in working with gay youth. The author calls for outreach to the gay client, support of the choice of a gay lifestyle as valid, the development of support systems of extended families.

Paroski, P. (1987). "Health care delivery and the concerns of gay and lesbian adolescents." *Journal of Adolescent Health Care, 8* (2), 188-192.

This article records the results of a study conducted with 121 gay and lesbian adolescents in New York City concerning their attitudes towards homosexuality in themselves and others and their use of mental health services. The results serve as a guide to the needs of gay youth to enable mental health professionals to do sensitive outreach to this community.

Robinson, K. (1991). "Gay youth support groups: An opportunity for social work intervention." *Social Work, 36* (5), 458-459.

This brief article calls for the creation of peer support groups for gay adolescents. The author develops the argument for support groups by focusing on gay youths' alienation due to the lack of parental, peer, and social supports, as well as the lack of ritual to celebrate their adoption of a gay identity.

Rofes, E. (1989). "Opening up the classroom closet: Responding to the educational needs of gay and lesbian youth." *Harvard Educational Review, 59* (4), 444-453.

This article discusses obstacles to the education of openly lesbian and gay youth in the public school system. The author examines Project 10 in Los Angeles and the Harvey Milk School in New York, two schools designed especially to meet the educational, emotional, and social needs of gay youth.

Saperstein, S. (1981). "Lesbian and gay adolescents: The need for family support." *Catalyst, 12,* 61-69.

This article examines the problems of gay youth rejected by parents and placed in residences and foster homes. The author examines the fact that many youth agencies in the San Francisco area will turn away gay youth, and the role of the Sexual Minorities Services Coalition in educating professionals in the needs of gay youth in an effort to change homophobic attitudes, encourage positive intervention, and to provide safe environments for this population.

Schneider, M. (1988). *Often invisible: Counseling gay and lesbian youth.* Toronto, Canada: Central Toronto Youth Services.

This work serves as a good introduction to beginning counseling with gay and lesbian youth. The first half of the book summarizes the development of social, legal, and psychological attitudes towards homosexuality and the

significance of gay youth within the gay/lesbian community.
The second half deals with counseling strategies.

Schneider, M., & Tremble, B. (1986). "Gay or
straight? Working with the confused adolescent." *Journal
of Homosexuality, 4*, 85-86.

An examination of the confusion over sexual identity
of the adolescent, this article offers guidelines for identifying
the adolescent experiencing confusion and strategies for
intervention. Also included are recommendations for the
worker experiencing difficulty in dealing with the question
of homosexuality.

Slater, B. (1988). "Essential issues in working with
lesbian and gay male youths." *Professional Psychology, 19*
(2), 226-235.

This article addresses the major issues affecting gay
youth. After summarizing etiological and developmental
issues, the author suggests some basic strategies in working
with gay youth. Of greatest value is the appendix of fiction
and nonfiction resources for lesbian and gay youth.

*Solocinski, M. (1990). "Ethical principles in the
counseling of gay and lesbian adolescents: Issues of
autonomy, competence, and confidentiality." *Professional
Psychology, 21* (4), 240-247.

This excellent article argues ethical issues in the
treatment of gay youth. Three specific cases are explored in
detail to demonstrate how competence is determined, thereby
necessitating confidentiality, respecting the autonomy of the
young gay client, or paternalistic sharing of the information
and parental involvement.

*Steinhorn, A.I. (1979). "Lesbian adolescents in
residential treatment." *Social Casework, 60* (3), 494-498.

This intelligent article examines lesbian behavior and
its implications in a residential setting. She differentiates

between homosexual occurrences and lesbian identity. She calls for sensitization to, education on, and acceptance of lesbianism by counselors, as well as the employment of lesbian and gay counselors as role models.

Sullivan, T., & Schneider, M. (1987). "Developmental and identity issues in adolescent homosexuality." *Child and Adolescent Social Work, 4* (1), 13-24.

This article examines developmental issues of the gay and lesbian adolescent. The authors use Diamond's model of sexual development, sexual identity, gender role and object choice, and various stage and cognitive theories of coming out.

Tremble, B. (1988). "Reference points: A qualitative examination of gay and lesbian adolescence." *The Social Worker, 56* (2), 68-70.

This Canadian article discusses the difficulties of growing up gay in a heterosexist society. The author explores the sense of "otherness" and isolation experienced by lesbian and gay youth and their need to find a vocabulary to discuss their sexuality and to come out.

Vergara, T.L. (1985). "Meeting the needs of sexual minority youth: One program's response." In R. Schoenberg, R. Goldberg & D.A. Shore (Eds.), *With compassion toward some* (pp. 19-39). New York: Harrington Park Press.

This article examines the program developed by the Eromin Center, Inc. to meet the needs of sexual minority youth. It focuses mainly on black males, but the guidelines could be applied to a similar population of lesbian youth of varied backgrounds.

Whitlock, K. (1988). *Bridges of respect: Creating support for lesbian and gay youth.* Philadelphia: American Friends Service Committee.
        This work outlines the major obstacles encountered by gay youth and the ways in which adults working with them can advocate for them. Of particular note is the section on resources describing organizations and books of value to gay and lesbian youth and their advocates.

Organizations

Hetrick-Martin Institute
(formerly, Institute for the Protection of Lesbian and Gay Youth, Inc.)
        112 East 23rd Street
        New York, NY 10010
        (212) 473-1157

Minnesota Task Force for Gay and Lesbian Youth
        100 North Oxford Street
        Saint Paul, MN 55104
        (612) 224-3371

National Network of Runaway Youth Service
        905 6th Street, N.W.
        Washington DC 20024
        (202) 488-0739

Sexual Minority Youth Services Coalition
        P.O. Box 1151
        San Francisco, CA 94101

DIFFERENTLY-ABLED LESBIANS

Brown, S., Connors, D., & Stern, N. (Eds.). (1985). *With the power of each breath: A disabled women's anthology.* Pittsburgh, PA: Cleis Press.

This is a good collection of articles by a wide range of differently-abled women, lesbians and non-lesbians. The articles run the gamut from humorous to sociopolitical essays.

Doucette, J. (1985). "Breaking the link of lies." *Resources for Feminist Research, 14* (1), 9-11.

This is a brief personal narrative by a differently-abled lesbian. She explains the feelings of isolation from community events which are not totally wheelchair accessible, as well as the problems encountered if one's disability is not immediately visible.

Doucette, J. (1989). "Redefining difference: Disabled lesbians resist." *Resources for Feminist Research, 18* (2), 17-21.

This article records the results of a survey with eleven disabled lesbians. The author explores the themes of discrimination due to disability in society at large and within the lesbian community and discrimination due to sexual preference among women with disabilities.

Franchild, E. (1990). "You do so well: A blind lesbian responds to her sighted sisters." In J. Allen (Ed.), *Lesbian philosophies and culture* (pp. 180-192). Albany, NY: State University of New York Press.

This first person account explores the feelings of a blind lesbian facing "ablist" oppression in their lesbian community. The writer calls on blind lesbians to work on their fears of disability, but more importantly, she stresses the need for able-bodied lesbians to support and participate in the disability rights movement.

Nestle, J. (1981). "The lesbian illness support group." Unpublished paper. (Available from The Lesbian Herstory Educational Foundation, Box 1258, New York, NY 10116).
This article describes a group of physically challenged lesbians and their lovers. The group functions as a support group, both physical and psychological, helping, at times, to accompany some to doctors, recognizing and dealing with anger, frustration and the terror that accompanies illness, death, etc. The message of strength and hope and constructive rage emanating from this article is an inspiration to workers to advocate for the physically challenged and to work towards change in current health policy.

Pies, C. (1985). "For disabled lesbians considering parenthood." In *Considering parenthood: A workbook for lesbians* (pp. 127-134). San Francisco: Spinsters, Ink.
This chapter offers a good examination of myths surrounding parenting by differently-abled lesbians. Exercises ask sensitive, reflective questions which help the differently-abled lesbian see the issue more clearly. Also discussed are the questions of caesarian section and parenting a disabled/able-bodied child.

*Rubin, N. (1981). "Clinical issues with disabled lesbians." *Catalyst, 12,* 37-45.
The author, a disabled lesbian feminist therapist, describes the experiences of her group for disabled lesbians, as well as the difficulty in identifying and doing outreach to this population. The author sees the therapeutic process as being one of grieving the loss of ability or able-ism.

Saxton, M. & Howe, F. (Eds.). (1987). *With wings.* New York: Feminist Press.
This collection of fiction and nonfiction selections by women with disabilities reflects the varied experiences of both heterosexual and lesbian women. The contributors

discuss societal oppression of differently-abled women as well as the impact of their particular disability on themselves, their friends, families, and lovers.

We are among you: Lesbians with disabilities (cassette recording). Minneapolis, MN: Radical Rose Recordings. (Available from Radical Rose Recordings, P.O. Box 8122, Minneapolis, MN 55403).

This tape offers a discussion by five differently-abled lesbians who belong to a gay disability group. Included are personal stories and critical examinations of many of the critical issues for this population: hospital visitation rights, employment, accessibility to recreation, cures, visibility, and attitudes of able-bodied people.

Wohlander, K., & Petal, M. (1985). "People who are gay or lesbian and disabled." In H. Hidalgo, T. Peterson, & N.J. Woodman (Eds.), *Lesbian and gay issues: A resource manual for social workers* (pp. 38-43). Silver Spring, MD: National Association of Social Workers.

This chapter deals with the need to confront the sexuality of disabled gays and their right to self-determination. The author examines homophobia and able-ism and their impact on self-esteem.

Organizations

Lesbian Illness Support Group
        Box 1258
        New York, NY 10001

Rainbow Alliance of the Deaf
        3007 Parkway
        Cheverly, MD 20785

RURAL LESBIANS

*Belitsos, G. (1983). "Rural gay and lesbian youth: Implications for youth workers." In S. Bergstrom & L. Cruz (Eds.), *Counseling lesbian and gay youth* (pp. 64-71). San Francisco: National Network of Runaway and Youth Services.

This article examines the situation of the gay youth in rural settings, where, due to extreme conservatism and a focus on the family, she/he is exposed to harassment/violence, rejection by family, and isolation.

*Breeze. (1981). "Lesbian social service needs and resources in rural communities." *Catalyst, 12,* 71-76.

This article examines the extreme isolation and potential distortion of self-image of lesbians in a rural community due to the abject homophobia in these family-oriented, fundamentalist communities. Needed are the support groups, advocacy for rights, and role models all of which will be facilitated by the coming out of gay professionals.

Cheney, J. (Ed.) (1985). *Lesbian Land.* Minneapolis, MN: Word Weavers.

This is a collection of personal accounts of lesbians living in collectives on the land. It helps one to see the needs, frustrations, and general dynamics of a good percentage of the rural lesbian population. These insights may be of utmost importance as more and more aging lesbians seek alternative forms of housing/sharing for their retirement. Many are choosing to live in collectives in rural areas.

D'Augelli, A. (1989). "Lesbian women in a rural helping network: Exploring informal helping resources." In

E. Rothblum & E. Cole (Eds.), *Loving boldly: Issues facing lesbians* (pp. 119-130). Binghamton, NY: Haworth.

This article explores the isolation of lesbians in a rural setting. The author presents the case of the rural lesbian women's organization in which the survey was conducted to determine the make-up of the women's support system, their general feeling of well-being, and the extent to which the organization played a significant role in facilitating affirmative relationships.

*Moses, A.E., & Buckner, J.A. (1982). "The special problems of rural gay clients." In A.E. Moses & R. Hawkins (Eds.), *Counseling lesbian women and gay men: A life-issues approach* (pp. 173-180). St. Louis, MO: Mosby.

The chapter on rural gays describes the isolation and utter fear of discovery in small, conservative communities. Given the lack of information, role models, socialization skills (as gays), many gays have internalized the negative stereotypes and further avoid trying to meet other gays. Social workers can disseminate information and plug the gay client into a support network.

Womanshare Collective. (1976). *Country Lesbians.* Grants Pass, OR: Womanshare Books. (Available from Womanshare, Box 681, Grants Pass, OR 97526)

The story of the creation of a lesbian collective this work helps to present the needs of the lesbian living off the land in a rural setting segregated from heterosexual society.

LESBIANS IN PRISON

*Faith, K. (1982). "Love between women in prison." In M. Cruikshank (Ed.), *Lesbian studies: Present and future* (pp. 187-193). Old Westbury, NY: Feminist Press.

This article reviews some "rules and regulations" of prison life supplemented by personal accounts of several lesbian prisoners.

Hansell, S. (1984).   "Behind bars: Juvenile institutions and lesbian youth." *Catalyst, 4* (4), 13-21.

This article examines the difficulties of the lesbian author's being "out" on the job with adolescent state offenders. It is a study of oppression due to gender, class, sexual orientation, and ageism. The author calls for the need to provide social workers who are sensitive to gay and lesbian youth.

*Jackson, D. (1978).   "Prison Ministry." In G. Vida (Ed.), *Our right to love* (pp. 171-173). Englewood Cliffs, NJ: Prentice-Hall.

This chapter examines the needs of lesbians in prison: advocacy, counseling, and alcohol and drug treatment. The author calls for greater outreach by lesbian organizations.

Leger, R. (1987).   "Lesbianism among women prisoners -- participants and non-participants," *Criminal Justice & Behavior, 14* (4), 448-467.

This study explores lesbianism in prison from the perspective of the "deprivation/importation" controversy. Those women who "imported" their lesbianism to jail are contrasted with those whose behavior developed in jail out of "deprivation" of sexual contact with males or affective contact in general. The study shows that the most criminalistic, feministic, aggressive, and homosexually active women were those whose homosexual behavior preceded their incarceration.

Propper, A. (1978).   "Lesbianism in female and coed correctional institutions." *Journal of Homosexuality, 3* (3), 265-274.

Based on responses to a questionnaire by 13 to 17 year old girls in an all-female and in a co-ed institution, the study examines rates and causes of institutional lesbianism. Results tend to rule out the "deprivation" model and reflect more of a previously established sexual behavioral pattern.

Shakur, A. (1978). "Women in prisons: How we are." *The Black Scholar, 9* (7), 8-15.
This article describes the lives of black women in prison with some pertinent remarks on lesbianism. The author examines the lack of understanding of lesbianism, as well as feminism in general in prison and focuses on the women's need for love, care, and mutual support.

Organizations

Gay and Lesbian Prison Project
        c/o Gay Community news
        167 Tremont Street
        5th floor
        Boston, MA 02111

No More Cages!
        P.O. Box 90
        Brooklyn, NY 11215

Prison Notes
        c/o Win Magazine
        326 Irvington Street
        Brooklyn, NY 11217

Prison Parole and Probation Program
        Gay Community Services Center
        Box 3877
        Los Angeles, CA 90038

OTHER MINORITIES

Beck, E.T. (Ed.). (1982). *Nice Jewish girls: A lesbian anthropology.* Watertown, MA: Persephone Press.

This anthology celebrates lesbian and Jewish identities. The essence of the book is a parallel between anti-Semitism and lesbian oppression.

Cruikshank, M. (Ed.). (1982). *Lesbian studies: Present and future.* Old Westbury, NY: Feminist Press.

This is an excellent guide to lesbian issues currently being discussed. The book covers the range of topics and materials to be explored in lesbian studies and women's studies courses. Also included are essays on the lesbian in academia, in the various disciplines and in various geographical areas. The resources are excellent.

Curb, R., & Manahan, N. (Eds.). (1985). *Lesbian nuns: Breaking silence.* Tallahassee, FL: Naiad Press.

This is a collection of personal accounts by lesbian nuns, some of whom still remain in the convent. It is a tribute to a courageous group of women who try to integrate their lesbian spirituality and sensitivity with their religion and its taboos on sexuality in general, and lesbianism, in particular.

Gregory-Lewis, S. (1978). "Lesbians in the military." In G. Vida (Ed.), *Our right to love* (pp. 211-215). Englewood Cliffs, NJ: Prentice-Hall.

This article offers practical advice on how to avoid discharge from the military for lesbianism. It examines the case for secrecy and that for gay rights activism.

III.
LESBIAN FAMILIES

FAMILY OF ORIGIN

Ashworth, A., & Back, G. (1984). "Parents helping parents." *Practice Digest, 7* (1), 11-12.

This article discusses groups run by parents of gays. Ashworth contends that it is inappropriate for social workers to run such groups; whereas, Back, a parent of a gay son, disagrees. A description of Back's six-session workshop on parents dealing with their children's gayness is included.

Back, G. (1985). *Are you still my mother? Are you still my family?* New York: Warner.

This is a personal account of a social worker whose son is gay. Writing with great empathy and charisma, Back discusses the emotional needs of parents of gays.

Becker, B. (1981). "Gays have parents too." *Catalyst, 12,* 105-109.

This article, written by the mother of three gays, and co-founder of the San Francisco Parents of Gays (P.O.G.), discusses the purpose of P.O.G. and its effectiveness in influencing legislators. The author recounts the personal story of her three children trying to get professional help and being treated as sick.

Bernstein, B. (1990). "Attitudes and issues of parents of gay men and lesbians and implications for therapy." *Journal of Gay and Lesbian Psychotherapy, 1* (3), 37-53.

This article examines the therapeutic issues of parents of lesbians and gays. The author addresses interventions used with parents as well as those with gay sons and daughters.

Berzon, B. (1979). "Telling the family you're gay." In B. Berzon & R. Leighton (Eds.), *Positively Gay* (pp.88-100). Millbrae, CA: Celestial Arts.

This article offers almost step-by-step advice on when, why, and how to disclose one's gayness to the family. The author suggests considering the quality of the relationship before disclosure and relating that to the reaction to the disclosure.

Borhek, M. (1983). *Coming out to parents: A two way survival guide for lesbians and parents.* New York: Pilgrim Press.

This is a practical guide dealing with the questions of how and what to disclose and what reactions to expect. The author also deals with the issue of grief and loss from the parents' point of view.

Carlson, H. (1984). "Some information for parents and families of lesbians and gays." Unpublished paper prepared for the Committee on Gay Concerns of the American Psychological Association. Washington DC: American Psychological Association.

This paper discounts myths surrounding the "sickness and cure" (medical) model of homosexuality. The author discusses the emotions experienced by the gay person and her/his parents upon the discovery of her/his gayness, and she recommends support groups and open communication. She astutely compares the parent who hides the child's homosexuality to the closeted daughter or son and the anxiety related to discovery.

Dahlheimer, D., & Feigal, J. (1991). "Bridging the gap." *Family Therapy Networker, 15* (1), 44-53.

    This article treats family therapy with families where one or more members are gay. The authors advise therapists to reach for the unspoken homophobia in the family of the gay person as well as in the gay person her/himself and to urge clients to develop other family-like networks. Methods of training heterosexual therapists to work with lesbians and gays are also discussed.

*DeVine, J. (1984). "A systemic inspection of affectional preference orientation and the family of origin." *Journal of Homosexuality, 2* (3),

    This article examines intervention with the family of origin of the lesbian/gay client. The author has developed a five-stage developmental model to maintain the functioning of the family system and to aid in the reintegration of the lesbian/gay member.

Fairchild, B. (1979). "For parents of gays: A fresh perspective." In B. Berzon & R. Leighton (Eds.), *Positively Gay* (pp. 101-111). Millbrae, CA: Celestial Arts.

    Written by a parent, this article deals with the typical fears of parents of gays and their feeling of isolation. She urges parents to believe their children when they disclose their homosexuality and to likewise believe that they are happy.

Fairchild, B., & Hayward, N. (1979). *Now that you know: What every parent should know about homosexuality.* New York: Harcourt Brace Jovanovich.

    Written by two parents of gays, the book offers practical advice on coming out as well as a discussion of the emotional reactions of parents. The coming out experience is told from both parents' and children's points of view.

Griffin, C.,   Wirth, M.,   & Wirth, A. (Eds.). (1986). *Beyond acceptance: Parents of lesbians and gays talk about their experience.* Englewood Cliffs, NJ: Prentice-Hall.

This work provides much needed information and support to the parents of lesbians and gays. It discusses the emotional stages experienced as one moves toward acceptance.

Hammond, T. (1984). "Support groups for parents of gays and lesbians." *Practice Digest, 7* (1), 9-11.

This article describes a support group for parents of gays. It discusses the need for parents to talk about their feelings of anger, denial, and loss.

Jones, C. (1978). *Understanding gay relatives and friends.* New York: Seabury Press.

A collection of personal narratives, the book deals with the question of homosexuality in significant others. Various relatives examine their feelings towards the gay member of the family, friend, teacher, etc.

Krestan, J. (1987). "Lesbian daughters and lesbian mothers: The crisis of disclosure from a family systems perspective." *Journal of Psychotherapy & The Family, 3* (4), 113-130.

This article addresses coming out as a lesbian to one's mother as an issue of differentiation where the principle therapeutic goal is to help the client disclose her lesbianism to her mother. Pertinent case material is presented.

Markowitz, L. (1991). "You can go home again." *Family Therapy Networker, 15* (1), 55-60.

This article treats the case of a lesbian and her father. Written as a first person account, this story tells of the reconciliation of father and daughter through therapy.

Pearlman, S. (1991). "Mothers' acceptance of daughters' lesbianism: A parallel process to identity formation." *Dissertation Abstracts International, 52,* 1733B.

This study examines 10 mothers of lesbians and the process by which they have come to accept their daughters' lesbianism. Having passed through stages of denial, anger, and loss, stages similar to those experienced by their lesbian daughters in coming out, these mothers eventually came to accept and mostly support their daughters' lesbianism. Similar, too, were the coping mechanisms used to come to this affirmative position: social support, affiliation, and self-disclosure.

Pogrebin, L. (1980). *Growing up free: Raising your kids in the 80's.* New York: McGraw-Hill.

This book contains an excellent chapter on homosexuality. It explores diverse myths and theories on the etiology of homosexuality and combats them in a gay affirmative manual on child-raising.

*Sauerman, T. (1984). *Coming out to your parents.* Pamphlet distributed by the Federation of Parents and Friends of Lesbians and Gays. Los Angeles: PFLAG. (Available from: PFLAG: P.O. Box 24565, Los Angeles, CA 90024).

This pamphlet examines questions to determine if the gay person is ready to come out to parents. The author discusses the existing climate at home, the certitude of the person, and the person's support system. The coming out process is compared to Kubler-Ross' five stages of loss.

Shernoff, M. (1984). "Family therapy for lesbian and gay clients." *Social Work, 29,* 393-396.

This article examines the use of family therapy in helping clients come out to their families of origin, children, etc. It also discusses legal risks where there may be a question of custody.   There is also a good discussion of family sculpting.

Silverstein, C. (1977).   *A family matter: A parent's guide to homosexuality.* New York: McGraw-Hill.
Written by a psychologist, this work offers support to parents and gays alike to deal with the homophobia which surrounds them.

*Wirth, S. (1978).   "Coming out close to home: Principles for psychotherapy with families of lesbians and gay men." *Catalyst, 1* (3), 6-22.
This article discusses therapy with the family of a gay client. The author presents a theoretical framework for the process which involves denial, confusion and guilt, acknowledgment of feelings and concerns, contemplation and decision-making, problem-solving, and acceptance.

Organizations

Parents and Friends of Gays
    PFLAG
    5715 16th Street, NW
    Washington, DC 20011

LESBIAN COUPLES

*Berzon, B. (1990). *Permanent partners.* New York: Plume Books.
This outstanding work studies the various structures of lesbian (and gay) relationships and functions as a quasi course in short-term couples counseling. Drawing from case material, the author, a psychotherapist, examines couples' communication,   power   imbalances,   internalized

homophobia, and traces these through the major areas of relationships: sex, money, legalities, children, in-laws, etc.

Blumenstein, P., & Schwartz, P. (1983). *American couples: Money, Work, and Sex.* New York: William Morrow.

This study examines four types of couples-- married, heterosexual non-married, lesbian, and gay male -- based on data from a 38-page questionnaire and from interviews. In addition, the authors relate the stories of five couples in each lifestyle.

Brown, L. (1986). "Confronting internalized oppression in sex therapy with lesbians." *Journal of Homosexuality 12,* (3/4), 99-107.

This article addresses the issue of sexual dysfunction in lesbian relationships. The author attributes this primarily to internalized oppression which views lesbian sexuality as all-dirty and all-good (as a reaction to stigma). She recommends therapeutic approaches which confront and redefine this oppression, as well as fixed definitions and forms of "lovemaking."

*Burch, B. (1982). "Psychological merger in lesbian couples: A joint ego psychological and systems approach." *Family Therapy, 9* (3), 201-207.

This article examines the issue of merger vs. autonomy as typically prevalent among women and, therefore, a very real problem for many lesbian couples. As women, both lesbians are less separate and seek greater intimacy because of the need to have their couple validated by society. There is, therefore, a further tightening of the bond, often leading to the development of a closed relationship. The author calls for a systems and individual approach to help the clients develop stronger ego boundaries and recapture intimacy.

Cabaj, R. (1988). "Gay and lesbian couples: Lessons in human intimacy." *Psychiatric Annals, 18* (1), 21-25.

    This article summarizes some of the basic issues for gay (and lesbian) couple formation and duration. Unfortunately, the emphasis (and stage theories) focuses on male couples. The "four dimensional matrix for evaluating couples" is quite helpful.

Caldwell, M., & Peplau, L. (1984). "The balance of power in lesbian relationships." *Sex Roles, 10* (7), 587-599.

    This article discusses the power balance in lesbian relationships. Although 97% of the respondents in this study favored equal power in relationships, only 60% said egalitarian relationships existed. The findings show that the greater the balance of power, the greater the satisfaction.

Clunis, D., & Green, G. (1988). *Lesbian couples.* Seattle, WA: Seal Press.

    This work studies lesbian couples in a very accessible, non-academic way. It examines various aspects and types of relationships and explores techniques for resolving conflicts at different stages of relationship building.

Decker, B. (1984). "Counseling gay and lesbian couples." *Journal of Social Work and Human Sexuality, 2* (3), 39-52.

    This article examines separation vs. fusion in the homosexual couple. The author explores ego boundaries in couples where society either ignores or transgresses these boundaries since there is no official validation by society of the homosexual couple.

Eldridge, N., & Gilbert, L. (1990). "Correlates of relationship satisfaction in lesbian couples." *Psychology of Women Quarterly, 14*, 14-36.

This study examines 275 lesbian couples concerning degree of satisfaction in their relationships based on autonomy, attachment, intimacy, and power.

*Elise, D. (1986). "Lesbian couples: The implications of sex differences in separation-individuation." *Psychotherapy 23* (2), 305-310.
This article reviews the literature on merging in lesbian couples. It attributes this merging to many causes: existence of the couple in a heterosexual society which does not validate a lesbian couple, pressure from the lesbian community to separate, as well as socialization as women. The author concludes that merging results primarily from the lesbians having been socialized as women who experience greater difficulties in separation-individuation issues.

Hall, M. (1978). "Lesbian families: Cultural and clinical issues." *Social Work, 23,* 380-385.
This article treats the lesbian couple or couple with children as the family unit. The author examines lesbian mothers and the necessity of involving the mother's lover as co-parent with the children. Hall sees the role of the social worker as supportive counselor and advocate, especially in custody cases.

Johnson, S. (1990). *Staying power: Long term lesbian relationships.* Tallahassee, FL: Naiad Press.
This work studies 108 lesbian couples. Chapters on particular couples are interspersed with chapters on thematic discussions, such as, sameness/difference, sexuality, children, family, friends.

*Kaufman, P.A., Harrison, E., & Hyde, M.L. (1984). "Distancing for intimacy in lesbian relationships." *American Journal of Psychiatry, 141,* 530-533.
This intelligent article examines the issue of merger in lesbian couples. The authors conceptualize the problem as

one of intimacy as a function of distance. Closeness develops, they say, as each partner takes her "space" within the relationship. Behaviors which are indicators of merger or fusion are sharing of friends, clothes, physical space, thoughts, etc. Therapeutic approaches focus on the "here and now" of the issue, including ego psychology's past and present mastery, system's recognition of social interactions and assertiveness training. This article is an almost "how-to" counseling manual.

Kirkpatrick, M. (1991). "Lesbian couples in therapy." *Psychiatric Annals, 21* (8), 491-496.
This article outlines the basic issues in therapy with lesbian couples. The author views the major factors differentiating lesbian couples from heterosexual couples as the socialization of both partners as women and society's lack of approval/support for the lesbian couple. She discusses merger, sexuality, custody issues, and aging.

*Krestan, J., & Bepko, C. (1980). "The problem of fusion in the lesbian relationship." *Family Process, 19,* 277-289.
This article examines boundary issues in lesbian relationships. As the boundary surrounding the lesbian couple in heterosexual society is either ignored, denied, or violated, both by the heterosexual, as well as by the lesbian community, many couples respond by building more rigid boundaries and merging. Lesbians in committed monogamous relationships may have to be helped to build stronger individual boundaries and to balance separateness and intimacy.

Krieger, S. (1983). *The mirror dance -- identity in a women's community.* Philadelphia: Temple University Press.
This work examines identity within the lesbian couple and in the larger lesbian community. Through direct

personal accounts, the author elicits from various lesbians experiences which demonstrate a tendency to merge within dyads and to refrain from differentiating oneself from the lesbian community.

*Lindenbaum, J. (1985). "The shattering of an illusion: the problem of competition in lesbian relationships." *Feminist Studies, 11* (1), 85-103.

This article examines the issue of separation-individuation in the lesbian couple. The author claims that a two-woman dyad is an unconscious tendency to re-create the primary intimacy between mother and child. This leads to merger and then, out of fear of loss of self, a forced separation or end to the relationship. The author recommends competition to remain individuated and, therefore, capable of growth and intimacy.

Lynch, J., & Reilly, M. (1986). "Role relationships in lesbian perspectives." *Journal of Homosexuality, 12* (2), 53-69.

This article represents the results of a study on equality in lesbian relationships. The findings show basic freedom from butch-femme roles. The greatest inequality seemed to exist in matters of intimacy. Also included is a good review of the literature on autonomy and attachment in lesbian relationships.

McCandlish, B. (1985). "Therapeutic issues with lesbian couples." In J.C. Gonsiorek (Ed.), *A guide to psychotherapy with gay and lesbian clients* (pp. 71-79). New York: Harrington Park Press.

This article explores the issues of trust and separateness in lesbian couples. It deals with women's tendency to bond and connect, not separate. The author claims that the overwhelming feeling of euphoria resulting from the (initial) intimacy of a lesbian relationship may dissipate once the relationship has existed for a while.

Mendola, M. (1980). *The Mendola report: A new look at gay couples.* New York: Crown.

This work is based on a nationwide study of 400 gay male and lesbian couples. The findings show that in most respects, gay and lesbian couples are similar to heterosexual couples. Likewise, the degree of stability of gay couples is reported to be equivalent to that of heterosexuals.

Peplau, L.,   Cochran, S.,   Rook, K.,   & Padesky, C. (1978). "Loving women: Attachment and autonomy in lesbian relationships." *Journal of Social Issues, 34* (3), 7-27.

This article examines the issues of dyadic attachment and autonomy among lesbians. The authors contend that these are not polar opposites, that one does not exclude the other. Autonomy is discussed as a phenomenon more prevalent in couples exposed to feminism.

Reilly, M., & Lynch, J. (1990). "Power-sharing in lesbian partnerships." *Journal of Homosexuality, 19* (3), 1-30.

This article reports on a study conducted with 70 lesbian couples to explore similarities in age, income, education, and finances among partners who characterized their relationship as egalitarian. Findings show that although egalitarianism is the ideal, it is not achieved in most cases.

*Roth, S. (1985). "Psychotherapy with lesbian couples: Individual issues, female socialization and the societal context." *Journal of Marital and Family Therapy, 2,* 273-286.

This article examines the uniqueness of the lesbian couple as being a partnership of two women, both of whom are committed to the relationship which receives no official validation by society. Socialized as women, both partners will have a struggle to maintain distance or separate ego boundaries where their primary socialization and lack of societal validation would push them toward fusion.

*Sang, B. (1984). "Lesbian relationships: A struggle toward partner equality." In T. Darty, & S. Potter (Eds.), *Women-identified women* (pp. 51-67). Palo Alto, CA: Mayfield.

      This chapter deals with issues in lesbian relationships ranging from role-playing to monogamy. The author examines the tendency to forget to "take for oneself" where both partners have been socialized as women. She also discusses the issue of friendships where the fine line between friend and potential lover is not clear.

Schrag, K. (1984, April). "Relationship therapy with same gender couples." *Family Relations*, pp. 283-291.

      This article is written specifically for straight counselors who wish to work with gay couples. The author outlines the basic issues of coming out, merging, finances, task management, monogamy, jealousy, and legalities of ownership. The author also advises counselors to examine their own issues over homosexuality and to resolve them first if one is to take on a gay client.

Tanner, D. (1981). *The lesbian couple*. Lexington, MA: Lexington Books.

      This work explores lesbian "marriage-type" relationships against a societal context which offers no validation of the lesbian couple.

Vida, G. (Ed.) (1978). *Our right to love*. Englewood Cliffs, NJ: Prentice-Hall.

      -- **Dilno,** J. "Monogamy and alternate lifestyles." pp. 56-60.

This author views monogamy as resulting from the lesbian's socialization as a woman in a heterosexual society. She also examines other forms of relationships.

-- **Whitlock, K.** "Striving towards equality in loving relationships." pp. 63-66.

This chapter discusses the inequalities within the lesbian community which result from the lesbian's socialization in a heterosexual society. The author examines role playing, self-effacement, and autonomy.

Woodman, N. (1982). "Social work with lesbian couples." In A. Weick & T. Vandiver (Eds.), *Women, power and change* (pp. 114-121). Silver Spring, MD: National Association of Social Workers.

This chapter offers a succinct view of certain issues peculiar to lesbian couples. These include unclear role expectations, conflicting vocational expectations, coming out, and sexual functioning. The author recommends enhancement of communication skills, building of self-esteem, and networking with lesbian support groups and other lesbian groups.

FAMILY OF PROCREATION

The Lesbian as Mother

Beck, E. (1983). "The motherhood that dares not speak its name." *Women's Studies Quarterly, 11* (4), 8-11.

    This article examines the difficult position of the lesbian mother torn between motherhood (with its assumption of heterosexuality) and open lesbianism (with the threat of losing one's job, one's support, custody). The authors also mention the fear of rejection by one's ethnic or religious group or by certain factions of the lesbian community.

*Berzon, B. (1978). "Sharing your lesbian identity with your children." In G. Vida (Ed.), *Our right to love* (pp.69-74). Englewood Cliffs, NJ: Prentice-Hall.

    This chapter examines how, when, and what to tell one's children about one's lesbianism. It suggests typical questions to anticipate. The author also offers suggestions on how to cope in an environment where mothers have to defend their mothering and children have to defend their mothers.

Bowen, A. (1991). Another view of lesbians choosing children. In B. Sang, A.J. Smith, & J. Warshow (Eds.), *Lesbians at mid-life: The creative transition*. San Francisco: Spinsters Press.

    This work is a first person account of one black woman's reflections on being a mother. She traces attitudes towards motherhood and parenting from her youth to the present, examining the prejudice of lesbian non-mothers towards mothers, and motherhood from heterosexual marriage as opposed to motherhood by artificial insemination. She also addresses the question of being black and lesbian.

*Bozett, F. (Ed.). (1987). *Gay and lesbian parents.* New York: Praeger.

   This collection of well-written articles by educators and mental health and legal professionals provides a comprehensive look at gay/lesbian parenting. It explores the particular issues of the parents, the children, and the families and, it draws legal and psychosocial implications.

Bozett, F., & Sussman, M. (Eds.). (1990). *Homosexuality and family relations.* New York: Harrington Park Press.

   This collection of articles written predominantly by health and mental health professionals explores the impact of homosexuality on families. Issues range from gay and lesbian youth and elders to the married gay male and adoption and foster care by gays and lesbians.

Crawford, S. (1988). "Cultural context as a factor in the expansion of therapeutic conversation with lesbian families." *Journal of Strategic and Systemic Therapies, 7* (3), 2-10.

   This article explores the case of two lesbians parenting a teenage girl. The author discusses various systemic approaches which consider the cultural context (homophobia) of the clients.

Corley, R. (1990). *The final closet,* Miami, FL: Editech.

   This gay parents' guide for coming out to children includes case material and a list of groups for gay parents.

Evans, B. (1990). "Mothering as a lesbian issue." *Journal of Feminist & Family Therapy, 2* (1), 43-52.

   This article examines the various issues involved in a lesbian's having children whether as a result of a previous heterosexual marriage or as a lesbian, through alternate insemination or intercourse. Cases are presented which exemplify the scenarios of the co-parenting couple, the step family, and the lesbian who has given up custody.

*Goodman, B. (1977). *The lesbian: A celebration of difference.* Brooklyn, NY: Out and Out Books.

This work consists of several essays which compare and contrast the lesbian and heterosexual mother. They explore issues of guilt vis-à-vis children and other issues in child development. The author discusses the need to work through the guilt where it exists and to garner support through support groups. She suggests that lesbian and gay social workers come out to act as role models.

Hanscombe, G., & Forster, J. (1982). *Rocking the cradle: A challenge in family living.* Boston: Alyson Publications.

This book is an informal study of the lesbian mother based on interviews conducted in England and Wales. Organized thematically, it examines the mother as lesbian, the lesbian as mother, children of lesbians, artificial insemination, and legal problems.

Huggins, S. (1990). "A comparative study of self-esteem of adolescent children of divorced lesbian mothers and divorced heterosexual mothers." *Journal of Homosexuality, 18* (1-2), 123-135.

This study examines 36 children aged 13-19 of divorced lesbians and heterosexual mothers for differences in self-esteem. Findings show significant statistical differences in self-esteem scores due to the double stigma of being in a divorced and lesbian-headed family.

Kirkpatrick, M. (1989). "Clinical Implications of lesbian mother studies." *Journal of Homosexuality, 14* (1-2), 201-213.

This article examines the key issues for clinical work with the lesbian mother. The author explores the various fears, doubts, and guilt experienced by the mother who tends to be judged by her sexual orientation and not by the quality of her mothering. The author recommends that the therapist deal not with the "deviance" of the lesbian but with family issues of trust, intimacy, separation/individuation, competition, and self-esteem.

Lamothe, D. (1989). "Previously heterosexual lesbian mothers who have come out to an adolescent daughter: An exploratory study of the coming out process." *Dissertation Abstracts International, 50,* 2157B.

This study explores the coming out process of ten women. While it was impossible to isolate the process of coming out to their daughters as separate from coming out to friends and other family members, all respondents expressed happiness at their honesty and integrity in coming out despite problems in so doing.

Levy, E. (1989). "Lesbian motherhood: Identity and social support." *Affilia, 4,* 40-53.

This article examines lesbian identity and social supports and the resultant capacity for tolerance for stress experienced in a homophobic environment. The 31 lesbian mothers interviewed received much support from lesbian and non-lesbian sources and exhibited positive lesbian identity.

Lorde, A. (1984). "Man child: A Black lesbian feminist's perspective." In *Sister outsider* (pp. 72-81). Trumansburg, NY: Crossing Press.

This chapter examines the role of the lesbian mother with a son. Lorde confronts the stereotypes of the lesbian mother in heterosexual society and her ostracism by lesbian separatist communities. She speaks of the strengths of the lesbian couple raising children. Children of lesbians are, according to Lorde, better able to deal with difference and oppression.

*Maggiore, D. (Ed.). (1992). *Lesbians and child custody*. New York: Garland.

This is a collection of the most pertinent articles of the last 15 years dealing with the personal, legal, and clinical issues involved in child custody for lesbians. The first section contains first-person accounts by lesbian mothers of their struggles with custody. The second examines studies to be used as expert testimony in court cases and material by therapists treating lesbian mothers and families. The last section contains a review of case law on the topic and strategies for presenting a case in court.

McCandlish, B. (1987). "Against all odds: Lesbian mother family dynamics." In F. Bozett (Ed.), *Gay and lesbian parents* (pp. 23-36). New York: Praeger.

This article is a developmental study of the lesbian family. It examines the stages in the dynamic of the couple from the pregnancy to the early development of the child. The author recommends strengthening the boundaries of the couple as well as those of the family in order to better cope with homophobia and to enhance the competence of the lesbian family.

Miller, J., Jacobsen, R., & Bigner, J.J. (1981). "The child's home environment for lesbian vs. heterosexual mothers: A neglected area of research." *Journal of Homosexuality, 7* (1), 49-56.

This article examines the results of a study of 34 lesbian mothers and 47 heterosexual and lesbian mothers. The findings show that lesbian mothers are less affluent and absent themselves more often from the home in order to work; yet, they are more focused on the child and developmental issues. The heterosexual mothers tend to be more "traditional" in their approach to their children and exercise a more traditional "authoritarian" control over them.

Mucklow, B. & Phelan, K. (1979). "Lesbian and traditional mothers' responses to adult response to child behavior and self-concept." *Psychology Reports, 44* (3), 880-881.

This article examines the results of a study to determine if significant differences between lesbian and heterosexual mothers exist on measures of natural attitude and self-concept. The results indicate no significant differences in self-confidence between the two groups.

*Pollack, S., & Vaughn, J. (Eds.). (1987). *Politics of the heart: A lesbian parenting anthology.* Ithaca, NY: Firebrand Books.

An outstanding collection of fiction and nonfiction, this work reflects the humanistic, psychological, legal, and political considerations of lesbians confronting motherhood. Of import is the politically assertive stance that lesbian clinicians and lawyers must not merely argue that lesbian mothering is "just as good as" that of heterosexual mothers, but rather commit to demonstrating the strengths and advantages of lesbian mothering and lesbian families.

Rafkin, L. (Ed.). (1990). *Different mothers: Sons and daughters of lesbians talk about their lives.* Pittsburgh: Cleis Press.

A sequel to *Different daughters,* this is a collection of stories written by sons and daughters of lesbians, some children of previous heterosexual marriages, others foster children or children by alternate insemination. While most interviews show a positive relationship between mother and child, some do explore confusion and difficulty, often resulting more from societal stigma rather than from conflict over the mother's choice. This book is an excellent beginning tool for the lesbian mother and her children to deal with the impact of her coming out.

Riley, C. (1988). "American kinship: A lesbian account." *Feminist Issues, 8* (2), 75-94.

This article, a progress report on the author's dissertation, explores ideas of kinship in our society and how lesbians are challenging the concept of family. After a review of anthropological theory on kin and family demonstrating the heterosexual bias which sees biology/affinity as the organizing principle of family, Riley describes the lesbian families interviewed as families of choice.

Romans, P. (1990). "Lesbian motherhood: The management of a dual identity." *Dissertation Abstracts International, 51,* 3239A.

This study explores the conflict inherent in the dual identity of lesbian and mother. The author examines the point in time at which these mothers took on their dual identity and the coping mechanisms they used to manage their identities.

Ross, J. (1988). "Challenging boundaries: An adolescent in a homosexual family." *Journal of Family Psychology, 2* (2), 227-240.

This clinical article is a case study of a lesbian family in which the teenage daughter of one partner acts out, jeopardizing the secrecy surrounding the (lesbian) family. A well presented study of sound therapeutic interventions, the article underscores the problems common to blended families as well as those peculiar to lesbian families.

Saphira, M. (1984). *Amazon mothers.* Ponsonby, New Zealand: Papers and Books.

Aimed at social workers, teachers, and psychologists, this work studies the results of 7 0 questionnaires completed by lesbian mothers in New

Zealand. It is an affirmation of their rights and experiences as lesbian mothers.

Schulenburg, J. (1985). *Gay parenting: A complete guide for gay men and lesbians with children.* Garden City, NY: Doubleday.

    Written by a lesbian mother, this book provides concrete suggestions and support to gay families through the author's experience and the experiences of others interviewed for this book. It covers coming out to one's children, custody, adoption, foster parenting, etc.

*Slater, S., & Mencher, J. (1991). "The lesbian family life cycle: A contextual approach." *American Journal of Orthopsychiatry, 6* (3), 372- 382.

    This article discusses family life cycle theory from the perspective of the lesbian family. The author stresses the effect of the lack of ritual and homophobia on the lesbian family and underlines the coping mechanisms employed by lesbians to counter them: a certain degree of fusion, involvement in the lesbian community, and creation of rituals to mark important events in the lesbian family life cycle.

*Steinhorn, A. (1982). "Lesbian mothers -- the invisible minority: Role of the mental health worker." *Women and Therapy, 1* (4), 35-48.

    This article serves as an overview of the lesbian mother and the major issues related to her lesbianism, her mothering, and her child's development. The author examines the importance of work for the lesbian mother, of child care, and the potential subsequent need to remain "closeted." She also briefly reviews some custody case law and outlines the major difficulties stemming from stigma for the children of lesbians.

Weston, K. (1990). *Families we choose: Lesbians, gays, and kinship.* New York: Columbia University.

This scholarly work by anthropologist Weston serves as an ethnographic study of gay families. Starting from the premise of gays as exiles from kinship where procreation or biology is seen as the organizing factor of "family," Weston argues the transformative effect of gay kinship, chosen combinations of lovers, lesbian and gay friends, adopted or birth children, etc., which alters the equation "straight is to gay as family is to no family" to "(blood) family is to chosen family." She addresses the issues of AIDS and alternate insemination and ends by defining gay families as incorporating notions of choice and biology.

The Lesbian and Childbirth

[S. & M.] Anonymous (1978). *Woman-controlled conception.* San Francisco: Union Wage.

This work is the personal story of two women who had children by artificial insemination by donor (AID). They offer advice on the various methods of insemination, other available options, and the advantages and disadvantages of each.

Egerton, J. (1990). "Nothing natural." *New Statesman & Society, 3,* 12-14.

This British article briefly discusses current legislation on donor insemination which while not directly barring access to insemination clinics by lesbians, does emphasize the child's need of a father. Case material is presented showing the stigma surrounding lesbians as mothers.

Fletcher, J. (1985). "Artificial insemination in lesbians." *Archives of Internal Medicine, 145,* 419-421.

This article examines the ethical considerations in a particular case of AID: the hospital's perspective, those of the various consulting physicians, and traditional religious ethics. The author concludes that physicians may ethically help lesbian couples with AID if a pattern of responsibility has been established.

*Gil de la Madrid, M. (Ed.). (1991). Lesbians choosing motherhood: *Legal implications of donor insemination.* San Francisco: National Center for Lesbian Rights.

This monograph, a revision of Donna Hitchen's 1984 work, is a current look at alternate insemination by donor for lesbians. It also includes a section on protecting the rights of the non-biological mother. Sample agreements are included.

*Goldstein, R. (1986, July 1). "The gay family." *The Village Voice,* pp. 19-28.

This article examines the new trends in gay families: ceremonies to validate the union, parenting by AID, adoption, etc. With this increase in coupling and parenting, comes a greater concern for concrete needs and rights: extending health benefits to cover children and "spouse equivalents," leave of absence to grieve the loss/death of a lover, inheritance rights, rights to act as adoptive/foster parents, etc.

Hanscombe, G. (1983). "The right to lesbian parenthood." *Journal of Medical Ethics, 9,* 133-135.

This article examines whether or not lesbians should be allowed to become mothers by AID The author considers differences in mothering (none) and differences in psychosocial development of children (none).

*Hitchens, D. (1984). *Legal issues in donor insemination.* San Francisco: Lesbian Rights Project.

(Pamphlet available from Lesbian Rights Project, 1370 Mission Street, 4th floor, San Francisco, CA 94103).

This pamphlet discusses the major legal issues in artificial insemination for a lesbian. Issues surrounding the rights of the natural father are also examined. All persons involved in AID are advised to write careful agreements, contracts, and nominations of guardianship to insure their rights. Sample contracts and agreements are included, as well as a bibliography of recent legal decisions relevant to AID.

Overall, C. (1987). "Sexuality, parenting, and reproductive choices." *Resources for Feminist Research, 16* (3), 42-45.

This Canadian article is a philosophical discussion of the question whether to allow lesbians and unmarried women access to artificial insemination. The author warns feminists not to argue that all women are entitled to bear children and that the government must provide every protection of that right. She holds that, on the contrary, one must contest the presumed necessity of a father (to co-parent) and challenge the alleged threat to family life inflicted by lesbians bearing children.

*Pies, C. (1985). *Considering parenthood: A workbook for lesbians.* San Francisco: Spinsters, Ink.

This book is a thorough examination of various issues surrounding parenting by lesbians. It describes different forms of parenting and assigns exercises to ascertain which, if any, is right for a particular couple or individual.

Rohrbaugh, J. (1989). "Choosing children: Psychological issues in lesbian parenting." *Women & Therapy, 8* (1-2), 51-64.

This article explores the choice of lesbians to parent. It addresses methods of pregnancy, co-parenting issues, birth, and the child's early development. The author examines the role of the co-parent and couple dynamics throughout the parenting process.

Wolf, D.G. (1984). "Lesbian childbirth and woman-controlled conception." In T. Darty & S. Potter (Eds.), *Women-identified women* (pp. 185-195). Palo Alto, CA: Mayfield.

This article discusses various aspects of alternative insemination for lesbians. In addition to pointing out the need for the inclusion of the mother's lover in the whole process from insemination to parenting, the author also examines the impact of the child's origin on his/her future dealings with peers and school personnel.

IV.
OPPRESSION

HETEROSEXISM IN THEORY

Arnup, K. (1985). "Lesbian-feminist theory." *Resources for Feminist Research, 12* (1), 53-55.

    This article examines radical, liberal, lesbian-feminist, and a "compulsory heterosexism" perspective based on Adrienne Rich's and Charlotte Bunch's theories. This theory holds that all institutions are based on the assumption that every woman wants to be bonded to a man both emotionally and economically. All who attempt to break out of the mold are labeled lesbian or deviant. A social control to protect male supremacy and the economic system, heterosexism makes male-female coupling inevitable. To keep women from discovering this form of social control, they are given the "illusion" of (heterosexual) sexual preference. In truth, there is no choice allowed.

Bayer, R. (1981). *Homosexuality and American psychiatry: The politics of diagnosis.* New York: Basic Books.

    This work examines the evolution of labels and attitudes toward homosexuality from sin to crime to disease. It, likewise, discusses the etiology and the various medical models leading up to the removal in 1973 of homosexuality from the *DSM*.

Conrad, P., & Schneider, J. (1980). "Homosexuality: From sin to sickness to life-style." In *Deviance and* *medicalization: From badness to sickness* (pp. 172-214). St. Louis, MO: C.V. Mosby.

This chapter treats the evolution of attitudes towards and the treatment of homosexuality from sin to crime to deviance (Freud) to pathology to lifestyle. The authors seem to imply that perhaps gays are more vulnerable now that they no longer have the "protection" that the label of sickness offered.

DeCrescenzo, T. (1985). "Homophobia: A study of the attitudes of mental health professionals toward homosexuality." In J.C. Gonsiorek (Ed.), *With compassion toward some* (pp. 115-136). New York: Harrington Park Press.

This is a discussion of a questionnaire surveying homophobia among mental health professionals. Generalizations are made concerning the hidden agendas of professionals trying to bolster their own heterosexuality or convert/seduce the homosexual. Guidelines for affirmative therapy are given, which, while innocuous, contain subjective and now (1986) questionable views on the etiology of homosexuality.

*Fontaine, C. (1982). "Teaching the psychology of women: A lesbian-feminist perspective." In M. Cruikshank (Ed.), *Lesbian studies: Present and future* (pp. 70-79). Old Westbury, NY: Feminist Press.

This chapter examines the feminist perspective on a psychology of women. Focusing on the concepts of patriarchy, heterosexism, institutionalized heterosexuality, and woman-identification, the framework brings insight into the psychology of women and women's studies. An excellent, concise study of heterosexism, this article erodes the myth of sexuality as the essence of lesbianism.

*Goodman, B. (1978). *Confronting homophobia.* New York: National Gay Health Coalition Education Foundation.

In this pamphlet, the author examines general myths concerning racism, sexism, classism, and heterosexism. She outlines a model for the acceptance of difference whether in heterosexuals or homosexuals: a model which allows for a nonjudgmental affirmation of diversity.

Goodman, B. (1980). *"Where will you be?" The professional oppression of gay people: A lesbian-feminist perspective.* West Hempstead, NY: J & P Distribution. (Available from AC 374 Woodfield Road, West Hempstead, NY 11552).

The essays include sketches of heterosexist myths behind multi-oppressions. The author examines the homophobia functioning within the social work profession. She discusses models for institutional change and her lesbian-feminist model of therapy.

*Gramick, J. (1983). "Homophobia: A new challenge." *Social Work, 28* (2), 137-141.

This article discusses homophobia as a culture-bound structure of our Western (American) culture. The author discusses the projected fears inherent in homophobia: fears of one's own potential homosexuality, fears of being converted, fear of destruction of family life, etc. She offers suggestions on how to combat homophobia from the "harmless" homophobic joke to the fight for a lesbian/gay to retain custody of a child.

Hammersmith, S. (1987). "A sociological approach to counseling homosexual clients and their families." *Journal of Homosexuality, 14* (1-2), 173-190.

Written by a sociologist, this article studies homophobia and internalized homophobia and attempts to debunk the myths leading to stereotypical views of homosexuals.

Hardesty, N. (1981). *God has no sexual preference: An open letter on homosexuality.* New York: Homosexual Community Counseling center. (Available from Evangelicals Concerned, Room 1403, 30 East 60th Street, New York, NY 10022).

This pamphlet is helpful in combatting biblical arguments against homosexuality. The author cites and explains biblical references against homosexuality.

*Herek, G. (1984). "Beyond homophobia: A social psychological perspective on attitudes towards lesbians and gay men." *Journal of Homosexuality, 10* (2), 1-17.

This article examines experiential, defensive, and symbolic attitudes against gays and suggests some methods of changing negative attitudes. For experiential, one might reinforce a positive attitude through exposure to more gays/lesbians; for symbolic, if based on religious values, one might present different interpretations more favorable to gays; for defensive, one might show that characteristics of gays do not necessarily threaten one's masculinity/feminity, role, etc.

*Neisen, J. (1990). "Heterosexism: Redefining homophobia for the 1990s." *Journal of Gay & Lesbian Psychotherapy, 1* (3), 21-35.

The author of this article examines the use of the words "heterosexism" and "shame due to heterosexism" as opposed to "homophobia" so as to better focus on the root of the problem: prejudice and power on the part of heterosexuals. Thus, he claims, one is better able to address issues of heterosexism both with gay and non-gay clients, while removing the stigma and anxiety from lesbians and gays and those who may be experiencing confusion concerning their sexual preference.

Norman, A. (1981). "The problem of violence." *Catalyst, 12,* 83-90.

This article examines violence as an expression of homophobia. The author describes various community groups formed for self-defense and/or counseling victims of violence specifically targeting lesbians or of rape in general. The need for counseling which includes the lover of the victim is also discussed.

Pharr, S. (1988). *Homophobia: A weapon of sexism.* Little Rock, AR: Chardon Press.

This book discusses sexism as the means to maintain the patriarchal relationships within American and Western cultures and targets homophobias as its most forceful weapon. The author establishes the connections between various oppressions: racism, classism, ableism, ageism, anti-semitism, etc. and calls for visibility of lesbians and collective (as opposed to individual) works of consciousness-raising, support and political action groups to combat these oppressions.

Rich, A. (1984). "Compulsory heterosexuality and lesbian existence." In T. Darty & S. Potter (Eds.). *Women-identified women* (pp. 119-149). Palo Alto, CA: Mayfield.

Rich's article exposes heterosexuality as oppression institutionalized to maintain the continuation of male dominance. In order for "heterosexism" not to be viewed as the social control it truly is, the myth of (hetero) sexual preference has been reinforced through the silencing of lesbian experience. Rich calls for the critical examination of heterosexism in order to undo patriarchal oppression as the "model for every other form of exploitation and illegitimate control."

Simpson, R. (1976). *From the closets to the courts.* London, England: Penguin Books.

This work is an exposé of the attitude towards and treatment of lesbians by religious, medical, and mental health institutions.

HETEROSEXISM IN PRACTICE

In the Courts - Custody

Achtenberg, R. (1987). *Lesbian and gay parenting: A psychological and legal perspective.* San Francisco: National Center for Lesbian Rights.
  This monograph examines and dispels myths used by the courts to deny custody to lesbian (and gay) parents. The extensive bibliography has been updated to 1989.

Achtenberg, R. (1991). *Preserving and protecting the families of lesbians and gay men.* San Francisco: National Center for Lesbian Rights.
  This monograph examines case law as it pertains to lesbians and gay men, including custody and visitation, rights of the co-parent, same-sex marriage, and partner benefits.

American Journal of Orthopsychiatry, 5 (3).

  -- **Hoeffer, B.** (1981). "Children's acquisition of sex-role behavior in lesbian-mother families." pp. 536-541.
  This article examines the results of a study based on play with children of lesbians and of heterosexual mothers. The findings show no significant cross-gender preferences for toys. Lesbian mothers seemed to be more flexible in choosing "neutral" toys. The author maintains that children are less influenced by mothers' preferences than by other models, especially television.

-- **Kirkpatrick, M.,   Smith, C.,   & Roy, R.** (1981). "Lesbian mothers and their children: A comparative survey." pp. 545-551.

This article examines the results of a study on the mental health of the children and mothers in lesbian households and in heterosexual women's households. The findings indicate no significant differences in the well-being of the children. The author claims that most lesbians divorce because of a lack of psychological intimacy in their marriages; heterosexual women divorce more because of alcoholism or abuse. In addition, lesbian mothers are more likely to share living arrangements and child care responsibilities with a live-in lover; this additional support seems to have a positive influence on the children.

Arnup, K. (1989). "Mothers just like others - Lesbians, divorce, and child custody in Canada." *Canadian Journal of Women and the Law, 3* (1), 18-32.

In tracing the evolution of divorce and custody law in Canada, the author attributes real power to the judge who determines whether the lesbian mother "deserves" to have custody of her child. She signals a liberalizing trend which, while granting that lesbianism in itself is not an obstacle, still judges a lesbian mother's appropriateness to be a mother on the degree to which her politics pose a threat to the role of women in a capitalist society.

Campbell, R. (1978).   "When one parent is a homosexual." *Judges' Journal, 17* (2), 38-41.

This article examines homophobia from the viewpoint of a United States Circuit Judge. Included are questions to determine "the best interests of the child." Campbell calls for limitations to the custody entrusted to a lesbian mother in order to safeguard the child on whom, he believes, the mother's homosexuality will have a detrimental effect in the long-term.

Darty, T., & Potter, S. (Eds.).   (1984).   *Women-identified women*. Palo Alto, CA: Mayfield.

     -- *****Gould, M.** "Lesbians and the law: Where sexism and heterosexism meet." pp. 149-163.

This article examines heterosexism and sexism in the legal arena. It elaborates on some recent divorce and child custody issues and points the way towards future legal battles over homosexuality.

     -- **Lewin, E.** "Lesbianism and motherhood: Implications for child custody." pp. 163-185.

This article examines the results of interviews with 60 women in the Bay Area (San Francisco) to compare lesbian and heterosexual mothers. Similarities include parallel support systems and inadequate child support. Lesbians are, however, more afraid to question this lack of support out of fear of retaliation or a challenging of custody. In general, this fear prevents many lesbian mothers from demanding their legal rights.

Di Lapi, E. (1989).   "Lesbian mothers and the motherhood hierarchy." *Journal of Homosexuality, 18* (1-2), 101-121.

This article establishes a conceptual framework from which to view the societal values acting as barriers to lesbian motherhood. The author states that a broadened understanding of institutional oppression can help professionals stop perpetuating this hierarchy.

Erlichman, K. (1989). "Lesbian mothers: Ethical issues in social work practice." *Women & Therapy, 8* (1-2), 207-224.

This article reviews the literature on lesbians and child custody and explores a few "ethical" issues in clinical practice.

*Falk, P. (1989). "Lesbian mothers -- psychosocial assumptions in family law." *American Psychologist, 44* (6), 941-947.

This excellent review of the literature on lesbian parenting and children of lesbians serves as a tool for expert witnesses and other professionals working with lesbian mothers. It addresses and dispels the negative assumptions concerning the lesbian mother and the well-being of a child in a lesbian mother family.

Gibbs, E. (1989). "Psychosocial development of children raised by lesbian mothers: A review of research." *Women & Therapy, 8* (1-2), 65-75.

This review of the literature focuses on studies concerning the well-being of the lesbian mother and the healthy development of her children. The author criticizes the methodology and scope of much of the research, seeking as it does to dispel misconceptions held by the general public. She calls for research which examines the strengths of the lesbian mother-child relationship.

Golombok, S., Spencer, A., & Rutter, M. (1983). "Children in lesbian and single parent households: Psychosexual and psychiatric appraisal." *Journal of Child Psychology and Psychiatry, 24* (4), 551-572.

This article gives the results of a study conducted in England on 37 children of 27 lesbians and 38 children of 27 heterosexual single mothers. The findings show no difference in the emotional well-being of the children. The authors conclude that being raised in a lesbian household did not per se lead to atypical development or constitute a psychiatric risk factor.

*Green, R. (1982). "The best interests of the children with a lesbian mother." *Bulletin of the American Academy of Psychiatry and the Law, 19* (1), 7-15.

This article examines the results of a study of 58 children raised by lesbians and 37 children raised by divorced heterosexual women. The author finds that the difficulties experienced by the children of lesbians stem from reactions to the divorce and not from the mother's lesbianism. According to Green, the "best interests" are best determined by the quality of the mother-child relationship and not by the sexual orientation of the mother.

Green, R., Mandel, J., Hotvedt, M., Gray, J., & Smith, L. (1986). "Lesbian mothers and their children: A comparison with solo parent heterosexual mothers and their children." *Archives of Sexual Behavior, 15* (2), 167-183.

This article discusses the results of a study with 50 lesbians and their 56 children and 40 heterosexual mothers with their 48 children to examine the impact of the mother's lesbianism on the child's psychosocial and psychosexual behavior. The authors conclude that there is no significant difference between the children of lesbian and of heterosexual mothers and that the "best interests" of the children should not be determined on the basis of the mother's lesbianism.

Harris, B. (1977). "Lesbian mother child custody: Legal and psychiatric aspects." *Bulletin of the American Academy of Psychiatry and the Law, 5* (1), 75-87.

Harris examines the prejudices of the courts against homosexuals: unfit as parents, they will expose their children to stigma, sexual perversion, and in the long run, they will convert their children to homosexuality. Judges feel that if custody is to be granted to a lesbian, severe restrictions must be placed on the conditions.

Harris, M., & Turner, P. (1986). "Gay and lesbian parents." *Journal of Homosexuality, 121* (2), 101-113.

This article examines the results of a study to determine if a parent's homosexuality created any special problems for the children. Few differences were found between the children of gays and straights. Although initially negative, the attitudes of the children to their parents' homosexuality were basically those of indifference or support (11 indifferent, 8 supportive, 5 confused, 1 angry, 1 ashamed, 1 hostile, 1 proud).

*Hitchens, D. (1990). *Lesbian mother litigation manual.* San Francisco: National Center for Lesbian Rights.

This manual acts as a step-by-step primer for those who wish to undertake a child custody case as the lesbian mother or as counsel representing her. Its clarity and thoroughness better enable the mother and counsel to assess the possibility of a successful case and therefore, the advisability of going to court.

Hunter, N., & Polikoff, N. (1976). "Custody rights of lesbian mothers: Legal theory and litigation strategy." *Buffalo Law Review, 25,* 691-697.

The author examines recent cases and concludes that in most custody cases involving a lesbian mother, the issue of homosexuality is the only consideration to determine the "best interests of the child." The authors suggest careful consideration of the potential consequences of litigation. The lesbian mother must decide what she is willing to do in order to remain "invisible": give up her lover, refrain from socializing in the lesbian community, etc.

Journal of Homosexuality, 5 (3).

-- ***Hitchens, D.** (1980). "Social attitudes, legal standards and personal trauma in child custody cases." pp. 89-95.

This article examines the major obstacles in winning/maintaining custody. These are the wide discretion in ruling by judges and the lack of binding past precedents.

The author recommends the education of lawyers and judges on issues of homosexuality.

-- *Nungesser, L. (1980).   "Theoretical bases for research on the acquisition of social sex roles by children of lesbian mothers." pp. 177-180.

This article reviews the literature on this topic and discusses how behavior is modeled in the context of the lesbian mother/child relationship. The author sets guidelines for the likelihood of a characteristic being modeled and based on these, believes that girls raised by lesbian mothers might tend to exhibit more androgynous behavior, that is, self-reliance, leadership ability, ambitiousness, self-assertiveness, and independence. The author calls for research to test this, as well as if and how it would be reinforced by the mother.

-- Pagelow, M. (1980).   "Heterosexual and lesbian single mothers: A comparison of problems, coping, and solutions." pp. 180-204.

This article examines the results of a study of heterosexual and lesbian mothers' responses to three concerns: custody, housing, and employment. Both groups report oppression in areas of freedom of association, employment, housing, and custody. The impact, however, of oppression is greater for lesbians. The author finds that as a coping mechanism to perceived oppression lesbians tend to develop higher levels of independence.

*Kleber, D.,   Howell, R.,   & Tibbits-Kleber, A. (1986). "The impact of parental homosexuality in child custody cases: A review of the literature." *Bulletin of the American Academy of Psychiatry and the Law, 14* (1), 81-87.

This article examines the most pertinent recent studies used to demonstrate the effect of a mother's lesbianism on her child. In general, the findings show no significant difference between the children of lesbian and heterosexual mothers. The authors recommend that the courts look at which parent would be more supportive of the welfare and growth of the child, and not at the parent's homosexuality.

Lewin, E. (1990). "Claims to motherhood: Custody disputes and maternal strategies." In F. Ginsburg & A. Lowenhaupt Tsing (Eds.), *Uncertain terms - Negative gender in American Culture* (pp. 199-214). Boston: Beacon.

This article explores the strategies used by women, including lesbians, to avoids custody challenges by their husbands: appeasement of their husbands, support by family and friends, and autonomy. The author claims that in the process of withstanding the challenge to her custody of the children, a woman's sense of motherhood is transformed from a natural (biological) attribute to one that has been self-consciously achieved.

*Lewis, K. (1980). "Children of lesbians: Their point of view." *Social Work, 25* (3), 198-203.

This article discusses interviews with children of lesbians, aged 9-26. Although there was some ambivalence in the expression of feeling toward their mother, these children accepted their mothers' lifestyle, were proud of their mothers' challenging society's rules and regulations and standing up for principles.

*Maggiore, D. (Ed.). (1992). *Lesbians and child custody.* New York: Garland.

This is a collection of the most pertinent articles of the last 15 years dealing with the personal, legal, and clinical issues involved in child custody for lesbians. The first section contains first-person accounts by lesbian mothers of their struggles with custody. The second examines studies to be used as expert testimony in court cases and material by therapists treating lesbian mothers and families. The last section contains a review of case law on the topic and strategies for presenting a case in court.

*Polikoff, N. (1987).   "Lesbian mothers, lesbian families: Legal obstacles, legal challenges." In S. Pollack & J. Vaughn (Eds.), *Politics of the Heart* (pp. 325-331). Ithaca, NY: Firebrand.

This article outlines the dilemma of lesbians and lawyers seeking custody for lesbian mothers: on one hand, the legal strategy of portraying the lesbian mother as no different from the heterosexual mother; on the other, the need to acknowledge the difference of lesbian motherhood in its challenge to the patriarchy in order to empower the lesbian and to maintain a vision of social change. The author examines various arguments for expanded rights for co-mothers; warns against the "equal rights" argument being co-opted by those who would deny lesbians custody; and argues for obtaining legal parenthood for both the biological and the non-biological mother.

Pollack, S. (1987). "Lesbian mothers: A lesbian feminist perspective on research." In S. Pollack & J. Vaughn (Eds.), *Politics of the Heart* (pp. 316-324). Ithaca, NY: Firebrand.

This article examines and analyzes studies comparing lesbian mothers with non-lesbian mothers. While the author acknowledges the value of such studies as a legal strategy to show that the lesbian mother is fit, she insists that the issue of difference not be overlooked. She speaks of the lesbian mother-child relationship as something unique and better able to instill in the child self-reliance and self-assurance.

Poverny, L., & Finch, W. (1988). "Gay and lesbian domestic partnerships: Expanding the definition of family." *Social Casework, 69* (2), 116-121.

This article calls for a redefining of the word "family" to reflect the changing statistics regarding new family groupings and to do away with automatic discrimination against gay and lesbian partnerships and families. The authors summarize those areas: custody, insurance, tax, etc., where gay couples face automatic discrimination because of policies based on the heterosexual, two-parent plus children model.

Quest, 5 (1).
-- **Agger, E., & Wyland, F.** (1979). "Wages due lesbians." pp. 57-62.
The article describes the work of Wages Due Lesbians in funding custody battles and in making referrals to sympathetic lawyers. This group is able to publicize a case and raise funds without divulging identities and to report victories through the media without names.

-- **Cole, G., & Pitell, J.** (1979). "National mothers' defense fund." pp. 62-69.
This article examines the issues involved in denying a woman custody on the basis of her lesbianism. The need for expert defense is obvious and costly. Lesbian Mothers' Defense Fund will help organize a campaign of fund-raising, media coverage, and legal expertise.

-- **Fitz-Randolph, J.** (1979). "A fund-raising strategy." pp. 69-72.
This article is almost a step-by-step "how-to" of fund-raising.

-- **Hunter, N., & Polikoff, N.** (1979). "Lesbian mothers fight back -- political and legal strategies." pp. 56-57.
Given the lack of precedent-setting in custody law, the authors contend that unless a custody case victory can serve as a tool for consciousness-raising in the lesbian community or as a tool to fight heterosexism, one victory remains an isolated, individual victory. It is therefore

difficult to raise funds for an individual case or to use it as a
rallying cause.

Rand, C., Graham, L., & Rawlings, E. (1982).
"Psychological health and factors the court seeks to control
in lesbian mother custody trials." *Journal of
Homosexuality, 8* (1), 27-39.

 This article discusses the results of lesbian mothers
who are "out" to their employers, their children, and the
community on the California Psychological Inventory and
Affectometer. The findings show a positive correlation
between the degree of overtness and their emotional well-
being. Yet, this openness of expression is precisely what
the courts want to curtail if lesbian mothers are to gain/retain
custody of the children.

*Rees, R. (1980). "A comparison of children of lesbian
and single heterosexual mothers on three measures of
socialization." (Doctoral dissertation, California School of
Professional Psychology, Berkeley, 1979). *Dissertation
Abstracts International, 40,* 3418B.

 This study compares children, 10 to 20 years old, of
12 heterosexual and 12 lesbian mothers. The findings
indicate that there is no significant difference between
children based on the mother's sexual preference and that it
is the total environment, not just the mother, which
influences the children.

Re Hatzopoulous. (1977). *Family Law Reporter, 4,*
2075.

 In this case, the courts granted custody to the partner
of the deceased lesbian mother. Although separated at the
time of the mother's suicide, the partner had remained in
contact with the child and was successfully awarded custody
over the context by the brother-in-law.

*Riddle, D. (1978). "Relating to children: Gays as role
models." *Journal of Social Issues, 34* (3), 38-58.

This article examines research on the development of sexual identity and sex-role behavior. Children, the author claims, make their own choices about sex-role behavior; they do not simply follow models. Acting as role models, gays and lesbians can help instill in their children an appreciation of diversity and, thus, aid in the healthy development of the child.

Rights of Women Lesbian Custody Group. (1986). *Lesbian mothers' legal handbook.* London, England: The Women's Press.

This work serves as a manual on custodial rights of lesbian mothers. It explains the legal system (in the United Kingdom) and how to proceed if custody is or is not contested. The work includes practical tactics to circumvent stigma attached to being a lesbian mother and to demonstrate the "best interests" of the child. Also included are the results of a survey of the outcome of 36 custody disputes, a review of case law in the U.K., Australia, and the U.S., and a brief annotated bibliography.

Rivera, R. (1979). "Our straight-laced judges: The legal position of homosexual persons in the United States." *Hastings Law Journal, 30,* 799-804.

This article presents a good review of case law on custody disputes with homosexual parents.

Stevens, M. (1978). "Lesbian mothers in transition." In G. Vida (Ed.), *Our right to love* (pp. 207-212). Englewood Cliffs, NJ: Prentice-Hall.

This article offers an excellent practical approach to divorce and custody. It examines an almost step-by-step process to help insure winning custody. Good resources are included.

Wyland, F. (1977.) *Motherhood, lesbianism, and child custody.* London: Falling Wall Press. [Available from Wages Due Lesbians] Women in Distribution, Box 8858, Washington, DC 20003).

This work discusses custody battles and strategies used by the Wages for Housework and the Lesbian Mothers Defense Fund in Toronto.

Organizations

Dykes and Tykes
        East Coast LMDF
        110 East 23rd Street
        Room 502
        New York, NY 10010
        (212) 441-3384

Lesbian Mothers Defense Fund
        P.O. Box 21567
        Seattle, WA 78111

Lesbian Mothers Resource List
        c/o Mary K. Blackmon
        2237 Glyndon Avenue
        Venice, CA 90291

Wages Due Lesbians
        c/o Brown
        100 Boerum Place
        Brooklyn, NY 11201

In the Workplace

Eversley, R. (1981). "Out on the job: A black lesbian-feminist takes a courageous stand -- an interview with Andrea Canaan." *Catalyst, 12,* 13-20.

This article examines the case of a black supervisor in the Louisiana Bureau for Women who was fired because of her lesbianism. Canaan was dismissed because she admitted her lesbianism-feminism at a board meeting.

Hedgpeth, J. (1979). "Employment discrimination, law and the rights of gay persons." *Journal of Homosexuality, 5* (2), 67-77.

This article reviews recent legal decisions in state/federal cases involving the rights of homosexuals in the public sector, the prevailing strategy has been to prove the "nexus," that is, the connection between the person's homosexuality and his/her inability to do the job. In the private sector and in such professions as teaching, great discretion on the part of employers (and judges) exists.

*Levine, M., & Leonard, R. (1984). "Discrimination against lesbians in the work force." *Signs, 9* (4), 700-710.

This article examines data collected from lesbians on job discrimination due to sexual preference. Their findings show that 60 percent anticipate discrimination; 24 percent actually experienced discrimination; 28 percent remain closeted as a coping mechanism. Although these figures are low, considering that they were raised in New York City, they do, in fact, support the claims of discrimination by lesbians and gay rights activists.

National Gay Task Force. (1981). "Employment discrimination in New York City: A survey of gay men and women." New York: N.G.T.F. (Available from The Fund for Human Dignity, 666 Broadway, New York, NY 10012, 212-529-1600).

This work examines the results of a study on discrimination against gays and lesbians at work. The findings show that 61 percent of the respondents believe their gayness would be a problem on the job if it were discovered; 39 percent believe it likely that they experience difficulty in getting a promotion; 21 percent acknowled actual discrimination.

Schneider, B. (1984). "Peril and promise: Lesbians' workplace participation." In T. Darty, & S. Potter (Eds.), *Women-identified women* (pp. 211-231). Palo Alto, CA: Mayfield.

This chapter examines the similarities of lesbians and women in general on the job. However, given the economic independence of lesbians, work tends to take on greater significance. Moreover, lesbians tend to try to integrate their work and social lives because of the difficulty of other social outlets.

Shachar, S., & Gilbert, L. (1983). "Working lesbians: Role conflicts and coping strategies." *Psychology of Women Quarterly, 7* (3), 244-255.

This article discusses inter- and intra- role conflict of the working lesbian. Interrole conflict is experienced as one over time spent working or with the lover. Strategies of coping involve negotiating and changing one's interpretations, leading to growth in self-esteem. Intrarole conflict is experienced as the fear of being discovered at work. Here, strategies are denial or avoidance, neither of which can be exercised without a substantial blow to one's self-esteem.

Valeska, L. (1981, January/February). "Double trouble for lesbians in the workplace." *New Directions for Women,* p. 11.

This article contains Valeska's, former director of the National Gay Task Force, testimony before the New York City Commission on the Status of Women concerning lesbians and the workplace. According to Valeska, there is double harassment, as women and as lesbians. Seen as fearful and uninterested in sex if she ignores sexual advances, she is often harassed, supervised in an overzealous manner, or ostracized. Valeska calls for a continued struggle to enact city and state gay rights ordinances and corporate nondiscrimination policies.

General Civil Rights

Arriola, E. (1988). "Sexual identity and the Constitution: Homosexual persons as a discrete and insular minority." *Women's Rights Law Reporter, 10* (2-3), 143-176.

This article argues the need for current legal strategies in gay related cases to go beyond the "right to privacy" argument. The author presents the "equal protection" argument and stresses the necessity of clarifying language and definitions related to homosexuals as a "discrete and insular" minority. She amply illustrates the development of her arguments with case law.

Bersoff, D., & Ogden, D. (1991).   "American Psychological Association Amicus Curiae briefs furthering lesbian and gay male civil rights." *American Psychologist, 46* (9), 950-956.

This article examines the cases in which the American Psychological Association has written Amicus Curiae briefs in support of gay civil rights: *New York v. Uplinger, Bowers v. Hardwick, Stover v. State*, and the Watkins and Ben-Shalom military cases. The authors explore the issues of right to privacy, equal protection under the law, and "equitable estoppel."

Eaton, M., & Peterson, C. (1988). *Andrews v. Ontario* (Minister of Health). *Canadian Journal of Women & The Law, 2* (2), 416-421.

This article reports on the decision in the Ontario (Canada) High Court of Justice not to grant long-term cohabiting lesbians with children the status of "spouses." The judge ruled against a violation of equality provisions since lesbians do not have "same (as heterosexuals) procreative capacities or family responsibilities."

Editors of the Harvard Law Review. (Eds.). (1990). *Sexual orientation and the law.* Cambridge, MA: Harvard University Press.

This work presents a thorough look at lesbian and gay men and the law. It examines employment, school, benefits, custody, and parenting. Issues, such as immigration and public accommodations are also discussed.

Ettelbrick, P. (1991). "Legal protection for lesbians." In B. Sang, J. Warshow, & A.J. Smith (Eds.), *Lesbians at midlife: The creative transition* (pp. 258-268). San Francisco: Spinsters Book Company.

This chapter is a succinct look at some legal options available to lesbians to protect their property and loved ones. The author discusses wills, joint property, cohabitation contracts, power of attorney, and living wills.

Granger, J. (1991). "'Outing' and freedom of the press: Sexual orientation challenge to the Supreme Court's categorical jurisprudence." *Cornell Law Review, 77,* 103-141.

This article explores the difficulty in arguing "outing" cases on the basis of defamation of character or invasion of privacy. Because "sexual orientation" is hard to define, therefore, to prove or negate, the author recommends an argument which demonstrates damage to reputation. As for privacy, the law must admit of an inviolate mental sphere where the press does not have the right to intrude.

Hitchens, D. (1982). *Lesbian rights handbook: A legal guide to lesbians.* San Francisco: Lesbian Rights Project.
　　This work covers the range of areas in which lesbians are guaranteed little or no protection under the law.

Kirk, M., & Madsen, H. (1989). *After the ball - How America will conquer its fear and hatred of gays in the 90s.* New York: Plume.
　　This controversial work outlines a plan for desensitizing heterosexuals to the fear of gays and lesbians and convincing them of the need to protect the rights of gays. While essentially advocating a media advertisement campaign, the authors go to great lengths to explain and attack past efforts to gain gay rights as ineffective and counter-productive. There are those who would find this work reactionary and self-deprecatory, (especially to gay men) as well as those who would fault its exclusion of lesbians beyond an occasional acknowledgment.

*Leonard, A. (1991). "From Law: Homophobia, heterosexism and judicial decision making." *Journal of Gay & Lesbian Psychotherapy, 1* (4), 65-91.
　　This excellent article dissects three court rulings against the rights of gays and lesbians to reveal the homophobia inherent in the discussions. *Bowers v. Hardwick, Padula v. Webster,* and *Constant A. v. Paul C. A.* are examined.

Meredith, D., & Wexler, E. (1983). "Lesbians and the right." *Resources for Feminist Research, 12* (1), 63-65.
　　This article examines the lack of protection under the law and the campaign against homosexuals by the political right. The authors are of the opinion that although it is dangerous to be out now, lesbians must stand out in order to stand together and fight for the rights which are their due.

Mohr, R. (1988). *Gays/Justice*. New York: Columbia University Press.

A philosophical consideration of gay rights, this well-written work discusses the ethics of a system of justice that maintains sodomy laws and the exclusion of gays from civil rights protections. Mohr stresses the fight for Dignity as opposed to individual "wins" and calls for civil disobedience as an ethical strategy.

N.O.W. *Lesbian rights: A woman's issue, a feminist issue*. (1980). New York: National Organization for Women.

These pamphlets cover diverse issues from biblical to economic. They provide a good historical overview and offer an invaluable source for refuting biblical prohibitions against homosexuality.

Schauber, F. (1985). "Some legal issues related to outside institutions." In H. Hidalgo, T. Peterson, & N. Woodman (Eds.), *Lesbian and Gay Issues: A resource manual for social workers*. Silver Spring, MD: National Association of Social Workers.

This concise article examines current cases in custodial law. Also included is information on power of attorney, wills, immigration, and licensure. The brief section on Criminal Law and AIDS should have been amended as of June 1986. The Department of Justice recommended that a private employer be allowed to fire someone with AIDS not on the basis of his/her disease per se, but because of the layman's (employer) ignorance of the disease and the fear of contagion to other employees.

*Siegel, P. (1991). "Lesbian and gay rights as a free speech issue: A review of relevant case law." *Journal of Homosexuality, 21* (1-2), 203-259.

This excellent article reviews case law relevant to lesbian and gay rights. The cases presented have all been argued as First Amendment cases: freedom of speech or association, non-verbal or symbolic expression, employment discrimination, sodomy laws, etc.

Vida, G. (Ed.). (1978). *Our right to love.* Englewood Cliffs, NJ: Prentice-Hall.
    The sections written by the Lesbian Law Section Collective and by J. O'Leary examine traditional and alternative measures to protect the interests of lesbians, within relationships and in society in general.

Warner, R. (Ed.). (1980). *A legal guide for lesbian and gay couples.* Reading, MA: Addison-Wesley.
    This work discusses various aspects of gay rights. There are sizable sections on wills and custody.

Organizations

Lambda Legal Defense and Educational Fund
        132 West 43rd Street
        New York, NY 10036

National Center for Lesbian Rights
        1663 Mission Street - 5th floor
        San Francisco, CA 94103

National Education Federation for Individual Rights
        c/o Lesbian Rights Project
        1370 Mission Street
        San Francisco, CA 94103
        (415) 441-2629

National Gay and Lesbian Clearing House
        Fund for Human Dignity
        666 Broadway

New York, NY 10012
(212) 529-1600

National Gay Task Force
    1517 U Street, N.
    Washington, DC 20009
    (202) 332-6483

National Lesbian and Gay Attorneys
    100 Boylston Street, Suite 900
    Boston, MA 02116

V.
HEALTH

GENERAL & GYNECOLOGICAL

*Brossart, J., & Pogoncheff, E. (1979, April). "The gay patient." *R.N.*, pp. 46-52.

      Pogoncheff's focus on "what not to do" with a gay client relates the story of a patient who did not receive quality care as a result of the homophobia of the staff assigned to this patient. Brossart's focus on "what you should be doing" calls for an examination of one's own fears of homosexuality, one's lack of knowledge of this population, and the perpetuation of false assumptions and/or judgmental behavior. She also recommends the taking of a psychosocial sexual history.

Chu, S.,   **Buehler, J.,**   **Fleming, P., & Berkelman, R.** (1990). "Epidemiology of reported cases of AIDS in lesbians, United States 1980-1989." *American Journal of Public Health, 80* (1), 1380-1381.

      This study of reported cases of AIDS among "women whose sole sexual partners" between 1980-1989 were women finds that 96 percent of these women were intravenous drug users. The study concludes that vaginal secretions and menstrual blood are potentially infectious, oral/vaginal exposure to these fluids can lead to HIV transmission, and that efforts to curb drug use in the lesbian community must be made.

*Darty, T., & Potter, S. (1984). "Lesbians and contemporary health care systems: Oppression and opportunity." In T. Darty, & S. Potter (Eds.), *Women-*

identified women (pp. 195-211).   Palo Alto, CA:
Mayfield.
    This article reviews the inherent sexism and
heterosexism of the male-dominated health industry.
Lesbians suffer double discrimination mainly as a result of
male-defined and imposed gynecological treatment geared
for the heterosexual women.   In addition, the authors
discuss the women's health movement, with its women-
controlled clinics and lesbian self-help and illness support
groups.

Fenwick, R. (1978). *The advocate guide to gay health.*
Boston: Alyson Books.
    This work contains some pertinent information on
endometriosis. The rest of the book is rather male oriented.
Moreover, the blatant sexism of the author on the topic of
rape as "seldom the worst thing that can happen to a person
physically" (p. 90) betrays the author's alleged sensitivity to
the lesbian issue.

Gillow, K. & Davis, L. (1987). "Lesbian stress and
coping methods." *Journal of Psychosocial Nursing, 25* (9),
28-32.
    This article reports on a survey of lesbians regarding
stressors and coping mechanisms.   The findings show
heightened stress due to homophobia and better coping skills
related to their level of involvement in a social network. The
authors, nurses, concluding that nurses must make an effort
to inform themselves about lesbianism, suggest further
implications for practice.

Good, R. (1976). "The gynecologist and the lesbian."
Clinical obstetrics and Gynecology, 19 (2), 473-482.
    This article examines the results of a study showing
little increase in studies, information, or updating of medical
literature on lesbianism in health care. The purpose was to
find out if gynecologists were aware of the presence of
lesbians among their clientele. Most gynecologists were not
aware of treating any lesbians.

Hepburn, C., & Gutierrez, B. (1988). *Alive and well*. Freedom, CA: Crossing Press.

 This general look at lesbian health includes non-traditional and traditional Western medical approaches. Topics include nutrition, sexuality, addiction, battering, and ageism, etc. Although there is much information on AIDS, it is not up-to-date and lacks specifics on safer sex for lesbians. Also now erroneous is the information on *tryptophan*.

*Hitchcock, J. (1989). "Bibliography: Lesbian health." *Women's Studies, 17*, 139-144.

 This bibliography is divided into the following categories: clinical observations, traditional psychiatric view, working with gay clients, attitudes of professionals toward homosexuals, research, lesbian attitudes toward health care, research reviews and research critiques.

Johnson, S., & Palermo, J. (1984). "Gynecological care for the lesbian." *Clinical Obstetrics and Gynecology, 27* (3), 724-733.

 This article examines the gynecological care and alcoholism among lesbians. It treats questions of disclosure from the perspective of both the practitioner and the lesbian client. Included are extremely helpful guidelines for practitioners dealing with undisclosed lesbians.

Messing, A., Schoenberg, R., & Stephens, R. (1985). "Confronting homophobia in health care settings: Guidelines for social work practice." *Journal of Social Work and Human Sexuality, 2* (2), 65-75.

 This article discusses the role of the social worker as advocate and educator in working with gay/lesbian clients seeking health care.

O'Donnell, M. (1978). "Lesbian health care: issues and literature." *Science for the people, 19* (3), 8-20.

This article discusses gynecological and mental health issues of concern to the lesbian. The author claims that the lack of information on lesbian gynecological needs, homophobia, and heterosexism have resulted in inadequate and insensitive delivery of service to the lesbian. Artificial insemination, as well as parthenogenesis is discussed.

*O'Donnell, M., Polock, K., Leoffler, V., & Saunders, Z. (1979). *Lesbian health matters!: A resource book about lesbian health matters.* Santa Cruz, CA: Santa Cruz Women's Health Collective.

This excellent general resource book provides succinct information on physical health matters. It includes good sections on alcohol abuse, gynecology, and feminist therapy.

Patty, C., & Kelly, J. (1990). *Making it -- A woman's guide to sex in the age of AIDS.* Ithaca, NY: Firebrand Press.

This short bilingual pamphlet discusses the most pertinent issues of AIDS and women, with additional information specific to lesbians. The section on resources is quite helpful.

Reyes, N. (1991, January 9). "Invisible science: Lesbians and AIDS." *Outweek*, pp. 12-15.

Addressing the invisibility of lesbians with AIDS, the author of this article explores the denial (that lesbians are at risk and are contracting AIDS) of the media, the medical establishment, and gay community-based health groups. According to Reyes, the resulting erroneous belief that lesbians are immune to HIV combined with differences of symptomatology rendering diagnosis more difficult in women serve to reinforce this invisibility, thus justifying the lack of studies, prevention campaigns, diagnosis, and treatment.

*Rieder, I., & Ruppelt, P. (Eds.). (1988). *AIDS: The women.* San Francisco: Cleis Press.

This collection of articles, personal accounts and essays, explores various issues of women dealing with AIDS: women with family members diagnosed with AIDS; women caregivers to persons with aids (PWAS); a woman whose PWA lover committed suicide, etc. One section concentrates exclusively on lesbians and AIDS, although there are several contributions by lesbians throughout the anthology.

Robertson, P., & Schachter, J. (1981). "Failure to identify venereal disease in a lesbian population." *Sexually Transmitted Diseases, 8* (2), 75-77
This article discusses gynecological needs of lesbians. The virtual absence of sexually transmitted diseases in exclusively lesbian women, yet, the normal-high range of cervical dysplasia would seem to indicate the superfluousness of routine screening for venereal disease in lesbians but the necessity of routine Pap smears.

Shaw, N. (1989). "New research issues on lesbian health." *Women's Studies, 17,* 125-137.
This article outlines the major areas of health concerns among lesbians. It discusses the significance of the underreporting of lesbians among women with specific illnesses, resulting in the lack of research with lesbians, and thus, the lack of service/treatment for them. The author lists breast and cervical cancer, HIV, chemical dependency, sexual abuse, battering, and mental health as major areas for research.

Smith, E., Johnson, S., & Guenther, S. (1985). "Health care attitudes and experiences during GYN care among lesbians and bisexuals." *American Journal of Public Health, 75* (9), 1085-1087.
This article represents the results of a study on lesbian health care. The findings show that 40 percent of the lesbian respondents fear that disclosure would result in

inferior care;   that 98 percent would prefer female gynecologists.

Stuntzner-Gibson, D. (1991). "Women and HIV disease: An emerging social crisis." *Social Work, 36* (1), 22-28.
This article explores social issues faced by women with HIV. The author addresses issues specifically related to women of color, lesbians, and prostitutes. Implications for practice are drawn.

Truppet, S., & Bain, J. (1990). "Preliminary study of lesbian health concerns." *Health Values, 14* (6), 30-36.
This article reports the results of a survey with 43 lesbians (1 celibate, 1 bisexual) concerning their use of and attitude towards the health care system. Findings show the greatest physical complaints to be gynecological along with relationship difficulties and depression. Respondents look for sensitive treatment and greater knowledge of lesbian issues in health care providers.

Organizations

Gay Nurses Alliance
St. Marks Clinic
44 St. Marks Place
New York, NY 10003
(212) 875-3136

National Gay Health Coalition
c/o Walter Lear
206 N. 35th Street
Philadelphia, PA 19104

National Gay Health Directory
National Lesbian and Gay Health Conference
P.O. Box 6189
San Francisco, CA 94101

MENTAL HEALTH

Alcoholism

*Anderson, S., & Henderson, D. (1985).   "Working with lesbian alcoholics." *Social Work, 30* (6), 518-525.

This article presents a good review of the literature and an intelligent discussion of intervention concerns. Although the focus of treatment must be on alcoholism and sobriety, treatment may also include coming out, role expectations, and parenting issues. The author discusses the approaches currently in use, as well as the role of the co-alcoholic and the lesbian community.

Black, C. (1990). *Double duty -- Gay-lesbian.* Denver, CO: MAC Publishing.

Part of the "double duty" series by Black, this book provides a general discussion of the problem (that of being a child of an alcoholic), and it explores the additional stigma (that of being gay, alcoholic, addicted to food, etc.). Black traces the secrecy and shame to the family disease of alcoholism which is further heightened by societal homophobia.   Recovery includes coming out as a COA (child of an alcoholic) and as a lesbian (or gay man).

Blume, E.S. (1985).   "Substance abuse: Of being queer, magic pills, and social lubricants."   In H. Hidalgo, T.L. Peterson, & H.J. Woodman (Eds.), *Lesbian and gay issues: A resource manual for social workers* (pp. 79-88).   Silver Spring, MD: National Association of Social Workers.

This article discusses the special circumstances surrounding the gay alcoholic; the role of the gay bar in socializing, the denial by the lesbian (gay) and the community of the alcoholism within it, and the invisibility of the lesbian alcoholic. The author recommends a systems approach to treatment with the focus on self-esteem.

Brunner, C. (1987). *For concerned others of chemically dependent gays and lesbians.* Center City, MN: Hazelden.

This pamphlet discusses the role of the co-dependent in the alcoholic process through vignettes of partners, parents, and friends of gay and lesbian dependents,

*Diamond, D., & Wilsnack, S.. (1978). "Alcohol abuse among lesbians: A descriptive study." *Journal of Homosexuality, 4* (2), 123-141.

This article examines the results of a study of dependency needs of fulfillment and power in the lesbian alcoholic. The findings indicate that the ten alcoholic lesbians with high dependency needs claimed no gratification of dependency needs through drinking. In drinking, they do, however, experience feelings of powerfulness. The author concludes that power, then, is the compensation for dependency needs and suggests that therapy should increase the lesbian's potential for power and effectiveness through a building of self-esteem and confidence. Additional emphasis is placed on assertiveness training and communication skills.

Diamond-Friedman, C. (1990). "A multivariant model of alcoholism specific to gay-lesbian populations." *Alcoholism Treatment Quarterly, 7* (2), 111-117.

This article calls for a model of gay-lesbian alcoholism which addresses psychodynamic and sociocultural issues. In briefly reviewing the literature, the author discusses stage theories of coming out and research on loss and dysfunction in the families of origin of gay and lesbians.

Fenwick, R. (1978). *The Advocate guide to gay health.* Boston: Alyson Books.

In the chapter on alcohol, great emphasis is placed on the role of the co-alcoholic. The author recommends that the co-alcoholic also be seen in therapy because of his/her potential need for the power/control that alcoholism accords him/her.

Finnegan, D., & McNally, E. (1987). *Dual identities: Counseling chemically dependent gay men and lesbians.* Center City, MN: Hazelden.

This work addresses the special counseling needs of those doubly stigmatized as alcoholics and lesbian or gay. The authors offer a synopsis of pertinent information of homosexuality, homophobia, incidence of alcoholism among gays, and psychological defenses common to alcoholics and "closeted" gays. They outline gay identity formation stages, and explore treatment issues and strategies specific to the gay/lesbian alcoholic.

Glaus, K. (1989). "Alcoholism, chemical dependency and the lesbian client." *Women & Therapy, 8* (1-2), 131-144.

This article reviews the literature on lesbians and alcohol/chemical dependency. The author discusses why the lesbian may be more at risk for dependency than a non-lesbian woman and recommends self-help groups such as Alcoholics Anonymous, Narcotics Anonymous, and Women for Sobriety as well as supportive therapy.

Gosselin, R., & Nice, S. (1987). *Lesbian and gay issues in early recovery.* Center City, MN: Hazelden.

This pamphlet offers support for gays in early recovery from alcoholism. Homophobia and the resultant stress are discussed. A companion pamphlet, *Gay and Lesbian alcoholics* is also available from the same press.

*Hall, J. (1990). "Alcoholism in lesbians: Developmental, symbolic interactionist, and critical perspectives." *Health Care for Women International, 11* (1), 89-107.

This article examines various perspectives on the development of alcoholism among lesbians. In addition to the sociocultural factors related to the stigmatized position of lesbians and the "isolationism" of the lesbian community, the author also considers genetic factors, the discrimination against women in general, and other "symbolic interactionist" concerns.

Holleran, P., & Novak, A. (1989). "Support choices and abstinence in gay/lesbian and heterosexual alcoholics." *Alcoholism Treatment Quarterly, 6* (2), 71-83.

This study explores therapeutic support choices made by gay/lesbian and heterosexual alcoholics in their abstinence. The respondents were residents in a private treatment center.

*Israelstram, S. (1986). "Homosexuality and Alcohol: Observations and research after the psychoanalytic era." *The International Journal of Addictions, 21* (4/5), 509-537.

This article serves as a review of the literature and research on alcohol and homosexuals. It lists the studies conducted since 1960, showing factors studied, methodology, findings, and implications for practice. The article offers little information on lesbians, and the interpretation of some of the studies mentioned would seem to be open to question.

Israelstram, S. (1988). "Knowledge and opinions of alcohol intervention workers in Ontario, Canada regarding issues affecting male gays and lesbians: Parts 1 & 2." *International Journal of the Addictions, 23* (3), 227-252.

This is a survey of alcoholism treatment specialists on attitudes and beliefs regarding gays and lesbians. In general, respondents believed that gays and lesbians drink more heavily than heterosexuals, that sexual orientation should be taken into account in treatment, that homophobia and lack of awareness/sensitivity discourage gays from coming for treatment.

Kominaro, S. (1989). *Accepting ourselves.* San Francisco: Harper.

This work is an analysis of the Twelve Steps of Alcoholics Anonymous specifically designed for gay and lesbian alcoholics. The author calls his work a "road map" for gay and lesbian alcoholics.

*Lewis, C., Saghir, M., & Robins, E. (1982). "Drinking patterns in homosexual and heterosexual woman." *Journal of Clinical Psychiatry, 43* (7), 277-279.

This article relates the results of a study comparing the drinking habits of 57 lesbians with those of 43 heterosexual women. The results show that 28-33 percent of the lesbians were problem drinkers and alcoholics compared to 5-7 percent of the heterosexual women. It also notes that of the 29 lesbians who did not frequent gay bars, 72 percent were problem drinkers and 38 percent were alcoholics. There is only one other empirical study on the drinking habits of lesbians (Fifield, 1975).

Martin, M. (1979). "The isolation of the lesbian alcoholic." *Frontiers, 4* (2), 32-35.

This article is a personal account of the struggle of a lesbian alcoholic to reach and maintain sobriety. She describes alcohol as the "wall" to protect her from the isolation and alienation she felt as a teenage lesbian. She calls on the lesbian community to reach out in support of the lesbian alcoholic and to create alcohol-free environments. Likewise, she recommends that alcohol counselors gain knowledge of lesbians and the lesbian community.

Mosbacher, D. (1988). "Lesbian alcohol and substance abuse." *Psychiatric Annals, 18* (1), 47-50.

This brief article explores the issue of lesbians and alcohol. The author reviews the literature and faults the studies with their qualitative and quantitative limitations. She finds no evidence to support the claim that alcoholism is a derivative of homosexuality and refers those with no awareness of lesbian issues to NALGAP, National Association of Lesbian and Gay Alcoholism Professionals, Gay Alcoholics Anonymous, and gay and lesbian hotlines.

*Nardi, P. (1982b). "Alcohol treatment and the non-traditional family structure of gays and lesbians." *Journal of Alcohol and Drug Education, 27* (2), 83-89.

This article discusses the three families of gays, the family of origin, the extended family or friends, and the couple, within the context of drinking and the gay bar. The extended family and the lover are considered as potential co-alcoholics by the author. He also examines the power imbalance and roles created by the alcoholism within the dyad.

*Neisen, J., & Sandall, H. (1990). "Alcohol and other drug abuse in a gay/lesbian population: Related to victimization?" *Journal of Psychology & Human Sexuality, 3* (1), 151-168.

This article records the results of an important innovative study examining the relation of sexual abuse, alcoholism, and homosexuality. Conducted by the Pride Institute, a treatment program for chemically dependent gays and lesbians, this study shows a high instance of sexual abuse among gay and lesbian substance abusers. The authors call for careful interviewing at intake (for treatment) to include instances of sexual abuse in the clients' histories so that treatment may then address this third stigmatizing factor, along with substance abuse and homosexuality.

Taylor, N. (1982a, April). "Alcohol abuse prevention: A community approach." Paper presented at the annual Alcohol Forum of the National Council of Alcoholism. Washington DC.

This paper is an examination of the similarity between lesbians and survivors of incest/domestic violence in their predisposition to alcohol abuse. The author claims that as a result of an inability to cope with conflicts between society's norms and the behaviors in their families or their own feelings, these women use alcohol to create the illusion of security, control, and trust. According to the author, the same community which fostered the development of this problem must help to solve it.

*Taylor, N. (1982b). "Community development as the primary network in the prevention of alcohol abuse among lesbians and gay men." Unpublished paper available from Alcoholism Center for Women, 1147 South Alvarado Street, Los Angeles, CA 90006.

This paper examines alcoholism as a symptom of the homophobic disease affecting the community. The author calls alcoholism the coping mechanism to deal with stigma, alienation, and denial of one's homosexuality. The community model of prevention includes networking to offer the support systems which combat alienation and stigma and education to train individuals to recognize denial and alcoholism as a mechanism to cope with anxiety. Training and education involve workshops and activities that address stress management, assertiveness training, relationship skills, etc.

Weathers, B. (1976). *Alcoholism and the lesbian community.* Washington DC: Gay Council on Drinking Behavior.

This concise pamphlet outlines the most important facts of lesbian alcoholism. It cites Fifield's statistics of 25-35 percent of the lesbian community as being affected by alcohol abuse, and attributes this to the stigmatized condition of the lesbian, the centrality of the lesbian bar in the community, and the lack of effective resources to help treat and/or prevent this problem. Implications for practice are given.

Zehner, M., & Lewis, J. (1985). "Homosexuality and alcoholism." In R. Schoenberg, R. Goldberg, & D. Shore (Eds.), *With compassion toward some* (pp. 75-90). New York: Harrington Park Press.

This article examines the need to focus directly on a gay client's alcoholism while also considering issues related directly to her/his homosexuality. The author traces the stages in coming-out along with developing dependency on alcohol.

Ziebold, T., & Mongeon, J. (Eds.). (1982). "Alcoholism and homosexuality" [Special issue]. *Journal of Homosexuality, 7* (4).

-- **Bittle, W.** "Alcoholics Anonymous and the gay alcoholic." pp. 81-88.
This article discusses the difficulties encountered by gays in straight AA groups. Bittle examines prejudices and narrow interpretations of the "12 Steps" by some older members, and shows that these are the alienating factors and not AA or the "12 Steps" per se. He suggests that gays be sponsored by other gay members or older trusted members or join a gay AA.

-- **Colcher, R**. "Counseling the homosexual alcoholic." pp. 43-51.
This article examines the similarities in the treatment of gay and heterosexual clients. The author discusses difficult areas for the gay client: initially revealing too much concerning his/her homosexuality, and then, having to deal with guilt. The author recommends talking about the feelings related to *being* gay and alcoholic in order to relieve some of the self-oppression. Moreover, he suggests that the counselor must help the client make decisions concerning being open about one's alcoholism and/or homosexuality on job applications.

-- **Driscoll, R.** "A gay-identified alcohol treatment program: A follow-up study." pp. 71-78.
This article examines the goals and outcomes of a gay alcohol treatment program within a gay treatment center. The clients who chose controlled drinking as a goal showed a 35 percent success rate; those who opted for total

abstinence showed a 26 percent success rate. The author suggests that one of the main goals of the program must be prevention through education: of the gay community concerning alcoholism and of alcoholism counselors concerning gays and the gay community. Included are the questions in the survey on alcoholic behavior.

-- *Mongeon, J., & Ziebold, T. "Preventing alcohol abuse in the gay community: Toward a theory and model." pp. 89-99.

This outstanding article explores alcoholism within the gay community. The authors discuss who is at risk and why, the rationale for the creation of programs within the gay community, and a model for alcohol abuse prevention. The group model almost creates a session-by-session agenda and concrete steps for attempting planned change of the drinking behavior in the gay community.

-- *Nardi, P. (1982a). "Alcoholism and homosexuality: A theoretical perspective." pp. 9-25.

Nardi discusses societal stigma, internalized self-hatred, and the resultant predisposition to alcohol abuse on the part of the lesbian or gay. Alcoholism is the denial mechanism for this self-hatred, as well as the illusion of safety within the emotional alienation.

-- Zigrang, T. "Who should be doing what about the gay alcoholic?" pp. 27-35.

Zigrang discusses the high rate of alcoholism within the gay/lesbian community and the lack of research/programs to deal with it. The author contends that it is not feasible to maintain exclusively gay treatment centers outside of large metropolitan areas. She also describes the setting up of a program for gays within a Veterans Alcoholic unit.

Organizations

Gay and Lesbian Alcoholism Services
P.O. Box 1141
Cooper Station
New York, NY 10276
(212) 713-5481

International Advisory Council for Homosexual Men and
Women in AA
P.O. Box 402
Village Station
New York, NY 10014

National Association of Lesbian and Gay Alcoholism
Professionals
204 West 20th Street
New York, NY 10011
(212) 807-0634

Pride Institute
14400 Martin Drive
Eden Prairie, MN 55344
1-800-54-Pride

Counseling and Therapy

General

*Boston Lesbian Psychologies Collective. (Eds.).
(1987). *Lesbian Psychologies.* Chicago: University of
Illinois.
        This excellent collection of articles touches on most
of the current issues in the lesbian therapy community. The
focus is on ethnic and cultural diversity with articles running

the gamut from questions of identity formation to couple and family issues to various therapeutic approaches.

Berger, R. (1977). "An advocate model for intervention with homosexuals." *Social Work, 22* (4), 280-283.

    This article discusses early interventions with gays and lesbians based on the medical model. The author calls for the development of an advocacy model to help support the adjustment necessary to maintain a homosexual orientation in a heterosexual culture.

Brown, L. (1989). "New voices, new visions - Toward a lesbian/gay paradigm for psychotherapy." *Psychology of Women Quarterly, 13*, 445-458.

    This article proposes an alternative model of psychological inquiry based on the experiences of gays and lesbians. This model would look at three elements which "cross-situationally" define a lesbian/gay reality: bisexuality, marginality, and normative creativity. Each element is applied to the understanding of dominant notions about human relationships.

Browning, C., Reynolds, A., & Dworkin, S. (1991). "Affirmative psychotherapy for lesbian women." *The Counseling Psychologist, 19* (2), 177-196.

    This article examines a variety of core issues of lesbians in therapy ranging from coming-out to sexual dysfunction. The authors make recommendations for future research.

Buhrke, R. (1989). "Lesbian-related issues in counseling supervision." *Women & Therapy, 8* (1-2), 196-206.

    This article explores various issues in supervision in the therapy of lesbian clients. Transference and countertransference issues between supervisor and supervisee and supervisee and client are discussed in the light of homophobia on the part of one or both or all.

Dulaney, D., & Kelly, J. (1982). "Improving services to gay and lesbian clients." *Social Work, 27* (2), 178-183.

In this article, homophobia among mental health professionals is examined as well as the lack of education concerning homophobia and the needs of homosexuals. Although the authors seem to place too much emphasis on sexuality, they do underline the need for more study on the aging gay, children of lesbian mothers and abandoned heterosexual spouse, where the burden of responsibility seems to be focused by the authors on the lesbian/gay client.

Escamilla-Mondanaro, J. (1977). "Lesbians and therapy." In E. Rawlings, & D. Carter (Eds.). *Psychotherapy for women: Treatment towards equality* (pp. 226-256). Springfield, IL: Thomas.

This chapter explores various issues in therapy with lesbians. The author differentiates between sexuality as an extension of one's self, as an expression of warmth and closeness, as an intimate encounter, and as copulation for reproduction; she holds that lesbianism is more than just a sexual issue. The pain experienced by lesbians stems not from the relationship, but rather from the constant fear of disclosure and/or the fear of rejection, alienation, and isolation. Finally, the author stresses the need for lesbian therapists to come out as lesbians to act as role models.

Falco, K. (1990). *Psychotherapy with lesbian clients -- Theory into practice.* New York: Brunner/Mazel.

Especially geared to the therapist who is not familiar with lesbian issues, this work serves as an introduction to the world of the lesbian and emphasizes the coming-out process and couple issues. Although primarily an elaboration of the professional literature on the topic, this book is a good example of lesbian-affirmative therapy.

Fassinger, R. (1991). "The hidden minority: Issues and challenges in working with lesbian women and gay men." *The Counseling Psychologist, 19* (2), 157-176.

This article examines basic issues of oppression and environmental obstacles to an affirmative gay identity. After summarizing past theories and practices related to gays and lesbians, the author suggests approaches to a gay-affirmative therapy.

Gambrill, E., Stein, T., & Brown, C. (1984). "Social services use and need among gay/lesbian residents of the San Francisco Bay area." *Journal of Social Work and Human Sexuality, 3* (1), 51-70.

This article discusses the results of a study on the needs of gays in the San Francisco area. The findings show that 71 percent of the respondents experience difficulty with straight counselors ranging from ignorance of gay issues to being labeled as sick. These findings support the general need for greater and better services to the gay community, as well as education and training of staff to work with a gay clientele, and the hiring of gay counselors.

Garnets, L., Hancock, K., Cochran, S., Goodchilds, J., & Peplau, L. (1991). "Issues in psychotherapy with lesbians and gay men: A survey of psychologists." *American Psychologist, 46* (9), 964-972.

This article records the results of a survey of psychologists' knowledge of biased or exemplary treatment of gay and/or lesbian clients. Findings show that 99 percent of those surveyed had heard of or had been party to biased treatment of gays, and some of those surveyed were aware of favorable treatment of gays in therapy.

Gerard, J., & Collett, C. (1983). "Dykes and Psychs." *Resources for Feminist Research, 12* (1), 47-50.

This article explores the experiences of lesbian social workers in a group of heterosexual and lesbian psychologists whose purpose was to exchange information on the needs for and the gaps in service delivery to lesbians. As a result, the lesbians felt the need to develop counseling collectives within the lesbian community where lesbian therapists could practice and/or serve as advocates who would sit in on sessions between lesbian clients and heterosexual therapists to insure that the client's lesbian identity would be respected.

Goldberg, R., & Schoenberg, R. (1981). "Defining gay social work: Beginnings with beginnings." *Catalyst, 12,* 77-82.

    This article examines the beginning of the gay project at Episcopal Community Services of the Diocese of Pennsylvania. Having ascertained that homophobia was the greatest difficulty in therapy between heterosexual therapists and lesbian and gay clients, the project directors set out to educate and sensitize other agencies to the needs of gays and to invite referrals.

Gonsiorek, J. (Ed.). (1985). *A guide to psychotherapy with gay and lesbian clients.* New York: Harrington Park Press.

    This collection of articles deals with lesbian and gay issues in psychotherapy. Of particular note are the chapters by Gonsiorek on diagnosis and Anthony on effectiveness and advantages of the lesbian therapist-lesbian client relationship. Gonsiorek's article is most helpful in differentiating between sexual identity crises and borderline or schizophrenic personality disorders.

Goodman, B. (1979). "An island of safety." *Practice Digest, 1* (4), 24-26.

    This article discusses the establishment of the Institute for Human Dignity, the first New York City counseling center to provide professional mental health services for gays and lesbians, as well as the program of services it offers. The author explores the need for therapy, as opposed to peer counseling, which sometimes suffices, for coming-out issues, relationship problems, poor self-image, and feelings of being constantly abused.

Groves, P., & Ventura, L. (1983, November). "The lesbian coming-out process: Therapeutic considerations." *Personnel and Guidance Journal*, pp. 146-149.

This article examines some of the fears of loss experienced by lesbians as a result of stigma: loss of one's job, one's friends, one's integrity.

Klein, C. (1991). *Counseling our own*. Seattle, WA: Consultant Services Northwest.

This work provides a history of the gay movement and mental health services and a rationale for the provision of services to gays. The author, a psychological and medical anthropologist, first examines the unmet needs of the gay community, needs which the community itself seeks to meet by creating gay and lesbian counseling services, and then studies, in depth, the Seattle Counseling Services for Sexual Minorities, the first of its kind to be founded (1968).

Kus, R. (1990). *Keys to caring*. Boston: Alysson Publications.

This compilation of articles covers a range of topics of concern to gays and their therapists. Issues are explored in such a way as to familiarize therapists (who have not knowingly worked with lesbians and gays) of the special needs of lesbians and gays.

Markowitz, L. (1991). "Homosexuality: Are we still in the dark?" *Family Therapy Networker*, *15* (1), 27-35.

This article addresses the issue of homophobia in therapy. The author explores transference and countertransference issues.

McDonald, H., & Steinhorn, A. (1990). *Homosexuality*. New York: Continuum.

This general guide to counseling lesbians and gay men acts as a good, basic introduction for non-gay practitioners to the world of gays and lesbians. The case vignettes and segments of process (therapeutic dialogue) are helpful as is the extended bibliography.

*Morrison, E. (1984). "Lesbians in therapy." *Journal of Psychosocial Nursing, 22* (8), 18-22.

The article examines the case of a lesbian couple against the framework of Bowen's theory of family therapy. According to the author, the therapist's role is one of investigation and data gathering and then of coaching the members of a system to ask their own questions concerning their behavior in order to think and problem solve rather than react according to old patterns. She sees the major potential problem in lesbian couples to be one of fusion.

Padesky, C. (1989). "Attaining and maintaining positive lesbian self-identity: A cognitive therapy approach." *Women & Therapy, 8* (1-2), 145-156.

This article applies cognitive therapy processes, which the author demonstrates to be consistent with a feminist model, to the question of coming out. In a collaborative effort with the client, the therapist is able to help her build her own experiences through guided discovery (Socratic questioning) to learn the source of her negative beliefs about lesbians and then, to analyze and accept or reject them.

Potter, S., & Darty, T. (1981). "Social work and the invisible minority." *Social Work, 26* (3), 187-192.

This is a good general overview of the special needs and characteristics of lesbians. The authors review some important studies which demonstrate the psychological well-being of lesbians.

Riddle, D., & Sang, B. (1978). "Psychotherapy with lesbians." *Journal of Social Issues, 34* (3), 84-98.

This article discusses how socialization as a woman impacts on lesbians. The authors discuss some characteristics typical of lesbians as opposed to the traditional woman, as well as the stress due to stigma.

*Roth, S., & Murphy, B.C. (1986). "Therapeutic work with lesbian clients: A systemic therapy view." In M. Ault-Riche (Ed.), *Women and family therapy* (pp. 78-89). Rockville, MD: Open Press.

This intelligent chapter examines the Milan systemic approach (as developed by Boscolo, Cecchin, Selvini, Palazzoli, and Prata) as a therapeutic approach with lesbian clients. The author explains the development of multiple hypotheses used in circular questioning to test, revise, and ultimately act as intervention to stimulate change in beliefs and behavior.

*Rothberg, B., & Ubell, V. (1985). "The coexistence of systems theory and feminism in working with heterosexual and lesbian couples." *Women and Therapy, 4* (1), 19-36.

This article compares and contrasts feminist and systems theories, examining areas of expected conflict. The authors outline some problems peculiar to lesbian couples, as well as those universal among both lesbian and heterosexual couples. They discuss how the therapeutic approach would differ in each couple and how feminism could be integrated in therapy with a resistant or non-feminist client or partner.

*Rothblum, E., & Cole, E. (Eds.). (1989). *Loving boldly: Issues facing lesbians*. New York: Harrington Park Press.

This volume is an excellent collection of articles relating to therapy by and for lesbians. Some of the issues examined are parenting, surviving sexual abuse, relationship violence, boundary problems in therapy and academia.

*Sang, B. (1977). "Psychotherapy with lesbians: Some observations and tentative generalizations." In E. Rawlings,

& D. Carter (Eds.), *Psychotherapy for women: Treatment toward equality* (pp. 266-279). Springfield, IL: Thomas.

This article examines important issues in therapy with lesbians. These issues include overcoming fear of isolation, of inadequacy in interpersonal relations since lesbians are not socialized along the lines of woman-to-woman relations, of an inability to meet and relate to people, and of an inability to be spontaneous because of constant filtration of feelings.

Siegel, R. (1987). "Beyond homophobia: Learning to work with lesbian clients." *Women & Therapy, 6* (1-2), 125-133.

This article relates the experiences of a non-lesbian therapist in familiarizing herself with the lesbian community and lesbian "reality" in an attempt to provide more sensitive and bias free services to her lesbian clients. Of particular note is her description of the therapeutic process in the lesbian couples group.

*Silverstein, C. (1991). *Gays, lesbians, and their therapists*. New York: Norton.

This work is a collection of 19 essays on various gay and lesbian therapeutic issues. Well respected lesbian therapists and lesbian issues are well represented in this volume. Issues range from bereavement and battering to Boston marriages and recovery.

*Sophie, J. (1982, February). "Counseling lesbians." *Personnel and Guidance Journal,* pp. 341-345.

This article examines the move from heterosexual socialization to a comfortable lesbian self-concept. According to the author, the therapist must not "push" the client to a too-early adoption of a lesbian label, since, in the client with low self-esteem, this may only result in an internalization of a negative stereotype. She recommends removing the negative evaluations of lesbianism first and then, those of self.

Stein, T. (1988). "Theoretical considerations in psychotherapy with gay men and lesbians." *Journal of Homosexuality,* 15 (1-2), 75-95.

This article examines general approaches to therapy and explores whether any particular approach is more conducive to successful therapy with lesbians and gays. The author discusses the homophobia of the therapist as detrimental to his/her gay clients and explores the general significance of the therapist's own homosexuality on therapy.

Whiting, D., Stewart, J., Feigal, J. & Silverberg, R. (1984). "What non-gay therapists need to know to work with gay and lesbian clients." *Practice Digest* 6 (3), 28-30.

This article examines the needs of the lesbian in therapy with a non-gay therapist. The authors stress the need for the therapist to resolve his/her own issues dealing with homosexuality and the ability to create a climate where, in the first session, the client feels comfortable enough to express her lesbian preference. Moreover, guidelines concerning stress, internalized stigma, expression of feeling, and support networks are given.

Wolfson, A. (1987). "Toward the further understanding of homosexual women." *Journal of the American Psychoanalytic Association,* 35 (1), 165-173.

This article reports on the proceedings of a panel on lesbians and psychoanalytic theory at the Annual Meeting of the American Psychoanalytic Association in 1984. Discussion centers around exploring new and broader interpretations of classical psychoanalytic theory regarding maternal drive and competence as organizing and motivating factors in psychological development. One case is briefly discussed. The non-pathological nature of homosexuality is reiterated.

*Woodman, N., & Lenna, H. (1980). *Counseling with gay men and women: A guide for facilitating positive life-style*. San Francisco, CA: Jossey-Bass.

This book is a concise, clear guide to counseling gay men and lesbians. The goal is self-actualization and the basic strategy is building on mastery, using this as motivation for further growth from identification of the conflict to problem-solving and mastery leading to enriched coping skills. The section on resolving sexual identity with the five stages of crisis is virtually a step-by-step manual on bringing a client through the identity crisis. The following section on promoting a positive self-image is also a practical counseling approach to change and growth. Counseling young gays is also dealt with most adeptly.

Specific Issues in Therapy

Battering

Duffy, D. (1991). "Battered lesbians: Are they entitled to a battered woman defense?" *Journal of Family Law, 29,* 879-899.

This article defines the battered woman syndrome, that of a woman who lives in such constant fear of abuse that she may actually attack her abuser at a time when he is not abusing her. Although this is not a defense of itself, it can be used with a plea of self-defense when expert testimony is given to explain the details of the life of the battered woman. Lesbians suffer as much, if not more, psychological trauma due to homophobia and their increased isolation. According to the author, their defense could be argued in a similar fashion.

Hammond, N. (1988). "Lesbian victims of relationship violence." Women & Therapy, *8* (1-2), 89-105.

This article examines the major obstacles to the successful diagnosis and treatment of battering in lesbian relationships and the actual cycle of abuse and its impact on their partners and their extended kinship network. After signaling the denial in the lesbian and therapy communities regarding lesbian battering, the author suggests various strategies and therapeutic interventions for positive change.

Kanuha, V. (1990). "Compounding the triple jeopardy: Battering in lesbians of color relationships." *Women & Therapy, 9* (1-2), 169-184.

    This article examines the three-fold stigma faced by lesbians of color involved in an abusive relationship due to the interface of racism, homophobia, and violence. It also discusses community response to lesbians of color and ethical issues in therapy.

*Klinger, R. (1991). "Treatment of a lesbian batterer." In C. Silverstein (Ed.), *Gays, lesbians, and their therapists* (pp. 126-142). New York: Norton.

    This chapter is an excellent case study of a lesbian batterer. The author describes her non-judgmental and supportive treatment of her client and guides therapists with the acuity of her therapeutic interventions.

*Leeder, E. (1988). "Enmeshed in pain: Counseling the lesbian battering couple." *Women & Therapy, 7* (1), 81-99.

    This clinical article describes three different types of lesbian battering: incidental abuse, chronic psychological abuse, and chronic physical abuse. Case material is used to illustrate each type, and well-developed treatment plans for the batterer, her partner, and the couple are discussed.

The Lesbian Caucus. (1990). *Voices of battered lesbians.* Available from: The Massachusetts Coalition of Battered Women, 107 South Street, 5th floor, Boston, MA G2111.

    This excellent tape explains the different forms of abuse perpetrated on lesbians by their partners, including homophobic abuse, dispels myths about mutual battering, addresses additional class and ethnic issues, and generally explores in-depth the psychology of battering. The didactic is interspersed with stories of battered lesbians of different ethnic, racial, and ability backgrounds.

Lie, G. & Gentlewarrier, S. (1991). "Intimate violence in lesbian relationships: Discussion of survey findings and practice implications." *Journal of Social Service Research, 15* (1-2), 41-59.

This article records the results of a study on relationship violence conducted with 11 lesbians at a music festival in 1985. Findings show a greater incidence of violence than previously acknowledged, similarities with violence in heterosexual relationships, however, a lack of sensitive personnel and service in agencies dealing with domestic violence.

Lobel, K. (Ed.). (1986). *Naming the violence.* Seattle, WA: Seal Press.

This work discusses the issue of battering within lesbian couples. Various authors expose the problem within the context of denial and silence on the part of individual lesbians and the lesbian community. Once again internalized stigma and homophobia are explored as contributing to the problem. Finally, the authors discuss themes and techniques for support groups and therapy groups, as well as methods and strategies for setting up shelters or safe spaces for battered lesbians and for sensitizing staffs of (heterosexual) battered women's shelters to lesbians and their special concerns.

Myers, B. (1989). "Lesbian battering: An analysis of power inequality and conflict in lesbian relationships." *Dissertation Abstracts International, 50,* 4229B.

This is a study of the relationship of power to violence and psychological abuse in lesbian relationships. Findings show that general difference between partners was not a good predictor of violence. The best predictor of violence was psychological abuse. When the respondent's partner made decisions by herself, and the respondent had overall "say" in the relationship, violence was predictable.

Renzetti, C. (1989). "Building a second closet: Third party responses to victims of lesbian partner abuse." *Family Relations, 38,* 157-163.

This article discusses the role of the service provider (including police, therapist, friends, etc.) in helping to prevent further abuse or in contributing to its perpetuation. Attitudes of service providers may reinforce the feelings of self-blame experienced by victims or support the victim in her rejection of violence and her attempt to escape. Recommendations for improvement of service delivery are made.

Schilit, R., Clark, W., & Shallerberger, E. (1991). "Intergenerational transmission of violence in lesbian relationships." *Affilia, 6,* 72-87.

This study reports on 46 lesbians involved in abusive lesbian relationships. Findings show significant associations between the respondents' experience of abuse in their families of origin and in their subsequent abusive lesbian relationships. Additionally, because shelters for abused women are unresponsive to the needs of lesbians, lesbians rarely use them, thus, the need for safe environments with sensitive (to lesbians) workers.

Schilit, R., & Lie, G.Y. (1990). "Substance use as a correlate of violence in intimate lesbian relationships." *Journal of Homosexuality, 19* (3), 51-65.

This article discusses problems of domestic violence and substance abuse in lesbian relationships. Respondents' frequency of drinking significantly correlated with committing abusive acts and also with being the victim of such acts. The author calls for an improvement in service delivery to lesbian batterers and victims and an exchange of knowledge/treatment skills between practitioners in the domestic violence and substance abuse fields.

Bereavement

Blume, E.S. (1984). "A bereavement group for lesbians." *Practice Digest, 7* (1), 27.

This article discusses the need for a separate bereavement group for lesbians since society is ignorant of both homosexuality and healthy mourning.

*Martin., A. (1991). "The power of empathic relationships: Bereavement therapy with a lesbian widow." In C. Silverstein (Ed.), *Gay, lesbians, and their therapists.* (pp. 172-186). New York: Norton.

This case study of a lesbian mourning the loss of her lover of ten years represents some of the clearest and most sensitive writing on the topic of bereavement, a topic understudied in the lesbian community, yet riddled with trite and often maudlin language in non-lesbian writings. The power of the author's presentation lies not only in her skills as a therapist, but also in her honesty and soul-searching in dealing with countertransference issues.

Moore, T. (1981). "Because she died . . . ." *Common Lives/Lesbian Lives, 2,* 42-49. (Available from P.O. Box 1553, Iowa City, IA 52244).

This is the personal account of the death of a lover. The article examines with great sensitivity the process of her lover's dying, surrounded by a group of lesbian friends and lovers. From it, one can learn of the practical and spiritual needs of the lesbian dying, of her lover, and her friends and how they interact and help one another. This is an excellent piece for information, motivation, and consciousness-raising in a support group on death and dying or for the social worker helping others through the death/dying process.

Nickerson, E. (1986). "The psychological experience of bereavement: Lesbian Women's perceptions of the response of the social network to the death of a partner." (Doctoral dissertation, Boston University, 1985). *Dissertation Abstracts International, 46,* 2566A.

This study examines the bereavement process of 15 lesbians who had lost a partner within a period from one to fifteen years. Results of the unstructured interviews show that it was primarily the friendship network which offered the support services normally extended by families. Other concerns revolved about anticipated interference prior to death in legal and medical decisions by the family of the deceased lover.

Couples/Intimacy

Carr, D. (1990). *Counseling same-sex couples.* New York: Norton.

This work examines couple therapy as understood by Carr with gay and lesbian couples. He incorporates elements of systems theory, Bowen, and manuchian models in treating gays and offers many case vignettes to illustrate his points.

*Green, G. (1990). "Is separation really so great?" *Women & Therapy, 9* (1-2), 87-104.

This excellent article explores the theories of Gilligan and Chodorow regarding women's inclination for connectedness in relation to the tendency of lesbian women in couples to "merge." The author discusses merger from a positive angle and contrasts it with fusion which she sees as indicative of a lack of ego boundaries within the relationship.

Mitchell, V. (1989). "Using Kohut's self-psychology in work with lesbian couples." In E. Rothblum & E. Cole (Eds.), *Loving Boldly: Isssues facing lesbians* (pp. 157-166). Binghamton, NY: Haworth Press.

This article examines the basics of Kohut's theories and applies them to determine healthy "self-object" functioning in a relationship. Case material is examined by the author who then outlines the advantage of using such a model as opposed to one which stresses merger/autonomy issues.

Pearlman, S. (1989). "Distancing and connectedness: Impact on couple formation in lesbian relationships." *Women & Therapy, 8* (1-2), 77-88.

This article adeptly explores distancing and intimacy in lesbian relationships without attaching the stigma usually associated with "merging." In avoiding the usual labeling as pathological of lesbians who tend to merge, the author allows the reader to see more clearly adverse effects wrought by societal oppression and the strategies used by the couple to adjust.

Rotenberg, L. (1989). "Impact of homophobia, heterosexism and closetedness on intimacy dynamics in lesbian relationships." *Resources for Feminist Research, 18* (2), 3-9.

This article studies intimacy and distancing in lesbian relationships in the light of homophobia. Merger, then, is not seen as pathological, but rather as protection from an aggressive environment.

Smalley, S. (1987). "Dependency issues in lesbian relationships." *Journal of Homosexuality, 14* (1-2), 123-145.

This article explores co-dependency in lesbian relationships. The author discusses general characteristics of co-dependents and, then, gives specific case material from couples therapy, and group therapy.

Wandrei, K. (1984). "Letting go and moving on: A support group for breaking up." *Practice Digest, 6* (3), 15-16.

This article discusses the formation of a group for breaking up. In the absence of a support system of family and friends, the ability to distance oneself from a lover who may have been one's total social and emotional support can represent a major crisis in a lesbian's life. The author gives examples of how some lesbians in her groups get help with the loneliness, isolation, and anger through her ten-session group process.

Eating Disorders

Rice, C. (1990). "Pandora's box and cultural paradox -- (Hetero)sexuality, lesbianism, and bulimia." *Resources for Feminist Research, 19*, 54-59.

This is an examination of eating problems as seen through the experiences of 4 lesbians and their interpretation of the relationship between weight and shape issues, (hetero)sexuality and power. According to the lesbians, bulimia may be an attempt to avoid marginalization and to resolve conflicts over power and body/body image.

Sex Therapy

Brown, L. (1986). "Confronting internalized oppression in sex therapy with lesbians." *Journal of Homosexuality, 12* (3/4), 99-107.

This article addresses the issue of sexual dysfunction in lesbian relationships. The author attributes it primarily to internalized oppression which views lesbian sex as all-dirty or all-wonderful. She recommends therapeutic approaches which confront and redefine this oppression, as well as fixed definitions and forms of "lovemaking."

Frye, M. (1990). "Lesbian 'sex'." In J. Allen (Ed.), *Lesbian philosophies and cultures* (pp. 305-316). Albany, NY: State University of New York Press.

In part a response to studies showing lesbians as having less sexual contact than heterosexual and gay male couples, this chapter explores the meaning and form of lesbian sex. Signaling the paucity of lesbian language to articulate things sexual, the author calls the creation of a vocabulary to talk about "what" lesbians do and believes this language will result from a greater willingness and freedom on the part of lesbians to talk about what they do sexually, freed from the influence of a male paradigm.

Hamadock, S. (1988). "Lesbian sexuality in the framework of psychotherapy: A practical model for the lesbian therapist." *Women & Therapy, 7* (2-3), 207-219.

This article outlines a basic model for helping a lesbian therapist integrate into the course of general therapy (not specifically treatment for sexual issues) examination of, education on, and modification of the sexual attitudes and behaviors of the client.

Loulan, J. (1988). "Research on the sex practices of 1566 lesbians and the clinical implications." *Women & Therapy, 7* (2-3), 221-234.

This article interweaves the results of Loulan's study of sexual practices of 1566 lesbians with her 10-year clinical experience as a sex therapist. Noteworthy is the discussion of the "willingness" model of lesbian sex: making a conscious effort to have sex as a treatment model for lack of desire and infrequent sex, issues common to many lesbians, single, involved in casual sex, or in a committed long-term relationship.

Loulan, J. (1990). *The lesbian erotic dance.* San Francisco: Spinsters Book Company.

This work explores lesbian sexuality in terms of butch-femme identities, and, in the process, examines the evolution of attitudes towards lesbian sexuality since the

1950s. While the sample used in this study is large (589 lesbians), the discussion and conclusions appear to be unrelated to the study and, therefore, unfounded.

Rothblum, E., & Brehony, K. (1991). "The Boston marriage today: Romantic but asexual relationships among lesbians." In C. Silverstein (Ed.), *Gays, lesbians, and their therapists* (pp. 210 -226). New York: Norton.

This chapter presents a case study of a fictitious couple, a composite sketch created by the authors to represent various aspects of the "Boston marriage," an asexual long-term relationship in which both partners consider themselves lovers. According to the authors, such couples usually see no problem with their asexuality and usually do not seek therapy until a break-up seems imminent. Intervention includes the exploration of it and why either partner has consciously chosen celibacy and if an asexual relationship responds sufficiently to the needs of both partners.

Sexual Abuse

*Bass, E., & Davis, L. (1988). *The courage to heal*. New York: Harper & Row.

This outstanding guide for women survivors of childhood sexual abuse functions as a quasi step-by-step process of recognizing and recovering from the abuse. Of particular note for counselors is the section entitled "For supporters of survivors." The final section contains personal accounts, resources, and an annotated bibliography.

Orzek, A. (1989). "The lesbian victim of sexual assault: Special consideration for the mental health professional." *Women & Therapy, 8* (1-2), 107-117.

This article examines the issue of treatment for the lesbian survivor of rape. The author explores the circumstances surrounding the rape of a lesbian and the subsequent discrimination due to her lesbianism, as well as to general societal stigma experienced by the victim of sexual assault.

Strapko, N. (1989). "Sexual preference of selected lesbians with a history of childhood heterosexual incest: A case study." *Dissertation Abstracts International, 50,* 2798A.

This study of four lesbians who reported childhood incest experiences examines their feelings concerning the impact of the incest on their lives. Three out of the four felt that the childhood incest did not cause them to choose a lesbian lifestyle.

Suicide

Saunders, J., & Valente, S. (1987). "Suicide risk among gay men and lesbians: A review." *Death Studies, 11,* 1-23.

This study explores the heightened incidence of suicide attempts among gays. (There are 2.5 to 7 times more suicide attempts among gays than among heterosexuals.). The author applies Durkheim's model for assessing suicide risk: alienation, lack of integration in society, and low anti-suicide defenses. With a heightened instance of alcoholism and greater interruptions in social connections, (gays are often estranged from biological family; gay relationships tend to be shorter lived than those of heterosexuals,), gays are more at risk for suicide. Given generally poor samples and research methods, the authors call for more and better studies and prevention efforts in the gay community.

Organizations

American Psychological Association
      1200 17th Street, NW

Washington, DC 20036
(202) 955-7600

Association of Lesbian and Gay Social Workers
110 East 23rd Street, #502
New York, NY 10010
(212) 777-7697

Commission on Gay/Lesbian Issues in Social Work
Education
1744 R Street, NW
Washington, DC 20036

The National Coalition Against Domestic Violence
2401 Virginia Avenue, NW
Suite 306
Washington, DC 20037
(202)293-8860

VI.
RESOURCES

BOOKSTORES

Giovanni's Room
      345 South 12th Street
      Philadelphia, PA 19107
      (215) 923-2960

Lambda Rising
      1625 Connecticut Avenue, NW
      Washington, DC 20009
      (202) 462-6969

Lammas Bookstore
      321 Seventh Street, SE
      Washington, DC 20003
      (202) 546-7292

Lesbian Herstory Educational Foundation (Archives)
      Box 1258
      New York, NY 10116
      (212) 874-7232

National Gay Alliance
      P.O. Box 38100
      Hollywood, CA 90038

(213) 463-5450

New Words Bookstore
      186 Hampshire Street
      Cambridge, MA 02139
      (716) 876-5310

Old Wives Tales
      1009 Valencia at 21st Street
      San Francisco, CA 94110
      (415) 821-4675

Womankind (mail order only)
      5 Kivy Street
      Huntington Station, NY 11746
      (516) 427-1289

PUBLICATIONS

Books -- General Resources

Bell, A., & Weinberg, M. (1978). *Homosexualities: A study of diversity among men and women.* New York: Simon & Schuster.
      This is a research study which compares and contrasts sexual experience, social adjustment, and psychological adjustment among lesbians and gay men.

The Boston Women's Health Collective. (1984). *The new our bodies, ourselves.* New York: Simon & Schuster.
      An updated, rewritten version of the original, this book includes some information on lesbians, among which are rural lesbians.

Human Rights Foundation. (1984). *Demystifying homosexuality: A teaching guide about lesbians and gay men.* New York: Irvington.

A resource book for guidance counselors and teachers in secondary schools, it represents the experiences of the Human Rights Foundation in training volunteers to speak in schools. It provides a curriculum for school personnel and parents and discusses some of the major issues of homosexuality.

Jay, K., & Young, A. (Eds.). (1979a). *The gay report.* New York: Summit.

The result of a survey of over 1,000 lesbians (and 4,000 gay men), this book is an expose of the variety of lifestyles and the diversity of the gay population.

Klaich, D. (1979). *Woman + woman: Attitudes towards lesbians.* New York: Morrow.

This work offers a general overview of attitudes towards lesbians in history, literature, and psychology. It also contains interviews with present-day (1979) lesbians.

Schwaber, F., & Shernoff, M. (Eds.). (1984). *Sourcebook on lesbian/gay healthcare.* New York: National Gay Health Education Foundation, Inc.

This book summarizes the proceedings and workshops of the First International Gay Health Conference in 1984. Essays written by prominent lesbians and gays in the social sciences and health fields review current literature, theories, and concerns in the major areas of lesbian and gay issues. The work also contains a good bibliography, lists of organizations, and health care professionals.

Newspapers and Directories

Au Courant
        319 South 12th Street
        Philadelphia, PA 19107

Black/Out, The magazine of the National Coalition of Black
Lesbians and Gays
        930 F Street, NW
        Suite 514
        Washington, DC 20004

Gayyellow Page, National Edition
        Renaissance House
        Box 292
        Village Station
        New York, NY 10014
        (212) 744-2785

Lesbian Connection (Acts as newspaper, bulletin board, and
communications network, especially for rural and isolated
lesbians. Contains list of contact persons across the world.)
        (order from Elsie Publishing)
        P.O. Box 811
        East Lansing, MI 48823
        (517) 371-5257

Maize: A lesbian country magazine
        (order from Word Weavers)
        Box 8742
        Minneapolis, MN 55408-0742

Off Our Backs
        1841 Columbia Road, NW
        Washington, DC 20009

The Open Door: Rural Lesbian Newsletter
       RR 2
       Box 50
       USK Store
       Terrace, BC V8G 3Z9, Canada

Plexus -- West Coast Women's Press
       545 Athol Avenue
       Oakland, CA 94606

Sappho's Isle
        960 Willis Avenue
        Albertson, NY 11507

Sojourner
       143 Albany Street
       Cambridge, MA 02139

Womanews
       P.O. Box 220
       Village Station
       New York, NY 10014

AUTHOR INDEX

TITLE INDEX

Journal articles appear in quotes.

245

ABOUT THE AUTHOR

DOLORES J. MAGGIORE is a graduate of the Sorbonne and earned her MSW from the State University of New York at Stony Brook. She has worked as a language teacher on the secondary level and as a school social worker. In addition, she maintains a private practice in psychotherapy, serving the gay and lesbian community. She serves on the Gay and Lesbian Concerns Committee of the National Association of Social Workers, New York State Chapter and has presented workshops at gay and lesbian conferences and anti-homophobia trainings. She has published articles on therapy and lesbianism in newspapers and edited volumes and edited a book on custody, *Lesbians and Child Custody: A Casebook* (Garland, 1992).